Jeane Kirkpatrick

AMERICAN WOMEN of ACHIEVEMENT

Jeane Kirkpatrick

PAT HARRISON

CHELSEA HOUSE PUBLISHERS

NEW YORK · PHILADELPHIA

Chelsea House Publishers
EDITOR-IN-CHIEF Remmel Nunn
MANAGING EDITOR Karyn Gullen Browne
COPY CHIEF Juliann Barbato
PICTURE EDITOR Adrian G. Allen
ART DIRECTOR Maria Epes
DEPUTY COPY CHIEF Mark Rifkin
ASSISTANT ART DIRECTOR Noreen Romano
MANUFACTURING MANAGER Gerald Levine
SYSTEMS MANAGER Lindsey Ottman
PRODUCTION MANAGER Joseph Romano
PRODUCTION COORDINATOR Marie Claire Cebrián

American Women of Achievement
SENIOR EDITOR Kathy Kuhtz

Staff for Jeane Kirkpatrick
ASSOCIATE EDITOR Ellen Scordato
EDITORIAL ASSISTANT Michele Haddad
PICTURE RESEARCHER Sandy Jones
DESIGNER Diana Blume
COVER ILLUSTRATION Bryn Barnard

1 3 5 7 9 8 6 4 2

Library of Congress Cataloging-in-Publication Data

Harrison, Pat.

Jeane Kirkpatrick, diplomat / by Pat Harrison.
p.   cm.—(American women of achievement)
Includes bibliographical references.
Summary: A biography of the woman who taught political
science at Georgetown University and served as the United
States ambassador to the United Nations during the Reagan
administration.
ISBN 1-55546-663-X
0-7910-0441-4 (pbk).
1. Kirkpatrick, Jeane J.—Juvenile literature.   2. Diplomats—
United States—Biography—Juvenile literature.   3. Women
diplomats—United States—Biography—Juvenile
literature.   [1. Kirkpatrick, Jeane J.
2. Diplomats.]   I. Title.   II. Series.
E840.8.K55H37   1991
327.2'092—dc20   90-2010
[B]   CIP
[92]   AC

CONTENTS

AMERICAN WOMEN OF ACHIEVEMENT

Abigail Adams
women's rights advocate

Jane Addams
social worker

Louisa May Alcott
author

Marian Anderson
singer

Susan B. Anthony
woman suffragist

Ethel Barrymore
actress

Clara Barton
*founder of the American
Red Cross*

Elizabeth Blackwell
physician

Nellie Bly
journalist

Margaret Bourke-White
photographer

Pearl Buck
author

Rachel Carson
biologist and author

Mary Cassatt
artist

Agnes de Mille
choreographer

Emily Dickinson
poet

Isadora Duncan
dancer

Amelia Earhart
aviator

Mary Baker Eddy
*founder of the Christian
Science church*

Betty Friedan
feminist

Althea Gibson
tennis champion

Emma Goldman
political activist

Helen Hayes
actress

Lillian Hellman
playwright

Katharine Hepburn
actress

Karen Horney
psychoanalyst

Anne Hutchinson
religious leader

Mahalia Jackson
gospel singer

Helen Keller
humanitarian

Jeane Kirkpatrick
diplomat

Emma Lazarus
poet

Clare Boothe Luce
author and diplomat

Barbara McClintock
biologist

Margaret Mead
anthropologist

Edna St. Vincent Millay
poet

Julia Morgan
architect

Grandma Moses
painter

Louise Nevelson
sculptor

Sandra Day O'Connor
Supreme Court justice

Georgia O'Keeffe
painter

Eleanor Roosevelt
diplomat and humanitarian

Wilma Rudolph
champion athlete

Florence Sabin
medical researcher

Beverly Sills
opera singer

Gertrude Stein
author

Gloria Steinem
feminist

Harriet Beecher Stowe
author and abolitionist

Mae West
entertainer

Edith Wharton
author

Phillis Wheatley
poet

Babe Didrikson Zaharias
champion athlete

CHELSEA HOUSE PUBLISHERS

"REMEMBER THE LADIES"

MATINA S. HORNER

Remember the Ladies." That is what Abigail Adams wrote to her husband, John, then a delegate to the Continental Congress, as the Founding Fathers met in Philadelphia to form a new nation in March of 1776. "Be more generous and favorable to them than your ancestors. Do not put such unlimited power in the hands of the Husbands. If particular care and attention is not paid to the Ladies," Abigail Adams warned, "we are determined to foment a Rebellion, and will not hold ourselves bound by any Laws in which we have no voice, or Representation."

The words of Abigail Adams, one of the earliest American advocates of women's rights, were prophetic. Because when we have not "remembered the ladies," they have, by their words and deeds, reminded us so forcefully of the omission that we cannot fail to remember them. For the history of American women is as interesting and varied as the history of our nation as a whole. American women have played an integral part in founding, settling, and building our country. Some we remember as remarkable women who—against great odds—achieved distinction in the public arena: Anne Hutchinson, who in the 17th century became a charismatic religious leader; Phillis Wheatley, an 18th-century black slave who became a poet; Susan B. Anthony, whose name is synonymous with the 19th-century women's rights movement and who led the struggle to enfranchise women; and, in our own century, Amelia Earhart, the first woman to cross the Atlantic Ocean by air.

These extraordinary women certainly merit our admiration, but other women, "common women," many of them all but forgotten, should also be recognized for their contributions to American thought and culture. Women have been community builders; they have founded schools and formed voluntary associations to help those in need; they have assumed the major responsibility for rearing children, passing on from one generation to the next the values that keep a culture alive. These and innumerable other contributions, once ignored, are now being recognized by scholars, students, and the public. It is exciting and gratifying to realize that a part of our history that was hardly acknowledged a few generations ago is now being studied and brought to light.

In recent decades, the field of women's history has grown from obscurity to a politically controversial splinter movement to academic respectability, in many cases mainstreamed into such traditional disciplines as history, economics, and psychology. Scholars of women, both female and male, have organized research centers at such prestigious institutions as Wellesley College, Stanford University, and the University of California. Other notable centers for women's studies are the Center for the American Woman and Politics at the Eagleton Institute of Politics at Rutgers University; the Henry A. Murray Research Center for the Study of Lives, at Radcliffe College; and the Women's Research and Education Institute, the research arm of the Congressional Caucus on Women's Issues. Other scholars and public figures have established archives and libraries, such as the Schlesinger Library on the History of Women in America, at Radcliffe College, and the Sophia Smith Collection, at Smith College, to collect and preserve the written and tangible legacies of women.

From the initial donation of the Women's Rights Collection in 1943, the Schlesinger Library grew to encompass vast collections documenting the manifold accomplishments of American women. Simultaneously, the women's movement in general and the academic discipline of women's studies in particular also began with a narrow definition and gradually expanded their mandate. Early causes such as woman suffrage and social reform, abolition and organized labor were joined by newer concerns such as the history of women in business and the professions and in politics and government; the study of the family; and social issues such as health policy and education.

Women, as historian Arthur M. Schlesinger, jr., once pointed out, "have constituted the most spectacular casualty of traditional history.

INTRODUCTION

They have made up at least half the human race, but you could never tell that by looking at the books historians write." The new breed of historians is remedying that omission. They have written books about immigrant women and about working-class women who struggled for survival in cities and about black women who met the challenges of life in rural areas. They are telling the stories of women who, despite the barriers of tradition and economics, became lawyers and doctors and public figures.

The women's studies movement has also led scholars to question traditional interpretations of their respective disciplines. For example, the study of war has traditionally been an exercise in military and political analysis, an examination of strategies planned and executed by men. But scholars of women's history have pointed out that wars have also been periods of tremendous change and even opportunity for women, because the very absence of men on the home front enabled them to expand their educational, economic, and professional activities and to assume leadership in their homes.

The early scholars of women's history showed a unique brand of courage in choosing to investigate new subjects and take new approaches to old ones. Often, like their subjects, they endured criticism and even ostracism by their academic colleagues. But their efforts have unquestionably been worthwhile, because with the publication of each new study and book another piece of the historical patchwork is sewn into place, revealing an increasingly comprehensive picture of the role of women in our rich and varied history.

Such books on groups of women are essential, but books that focus on the lives of individuals are equally indispensable. Biographies can be inspirational, offering their readers the example of people with vision who have looked outside themselves for their goals and have often struggled against great obstacles to achieve them. Marian Anderson, for instance, had to overcome racial bigotry in order to perfect her art and perform as a concert singer. Isadora Duncan defied the rules of classical dance to find true artistic freedom. Jane Addams had to break down society's notions of the proper role for women in order to create new social institutions, notably the settlement house. All of these women had to come to terms both with themselves and with the world in which they lived. Only then could they move ahead as pioneers in their chosen callings.

Biography can inspire not only by adulation but also by realism. It helps us to see not only the qualities in others that we hope to emulate but also, perhaps, the weaknesses that made them "human." By helping us identify with the subject on a more personal level they help us to feel that we, too, can achieve such goals. We read about Eleanor Roosevelt, for example, who occupied a unique and seemingly enviable position as the wife of the president. Yet we can sympathize with her inner dilemma: an inherently shy woman who had to force herself to live a most public life in order to use her position to benefit others. We may not be able to imagine ourselves having the immense poetic talent of Emily Dickinson, but from her story we can understand the challenges faced by a creative woman who was expected to fulfill many family responsibilities. And though few of us will ever reach the level of athletic accomplishment displayed by Wilma Rudolph or Babe Zaharias, we can still appreciate their spirit, their overwhelming will to excel.

A biography is a multifaceted lens. It is first of all a magnification, the intimate examination of one particular life. But at the same time, it is a wide-angle lens, informing us about the world in which the subject lived. We come away from reading about one life knowing more about the social, political, and economic fabric of the time. It is for this reason, perhaps, that the great New England essayist Ralph Waldo Emerson wrote, in 1841, "There is properly no history: only biography." And it is also why biography, and particularly women's biography, will continue to fascinate writers and readers alike.

Jeane Kirkpatrick

As a Georgetown professor, a UN ambassador, an author, and a respected foreign affairs analyst, Jeane Kirkpatrick has had an enormous influence on how the world views the United States—and how U.S. leaders view the rest of the world.

ONE

Crossing a Rubicon

On April 1, 1980, Jeane Kirkpatrick received a momentous phone call. She later found the date—April Fools' Day—rather humorous, but at the time she did not give it a thought, for she was getting some much-needed rest in bed after she had come down with a fever upon returning from a trip to southern India. There she had represented the United States Information Agency—which conducts the U.S. government's informational, educational, and cultural programs in foreign countries—and delivered a lecture about the American political system at the official opening of a national library in the city of Hyderabad. Lecturing came easily to Kirkpatrick, for she was a professor. But her job would change. When she picked up the telephone that day, she began a chain of events that would sweep her out of the academic world and plunge her directly into the maelstrom of American and international politics.

On the other end of the line was Richard V. Allen, an adviser to the Republican party's candidate for president, Ronald Reagan. Then the governor of California, Reagan was running against Jimmy Carter, the current president. Allen told Kirkpatrick that the governor would like to meet her. Could they arrange an appointment?

Kirkpatrick knew very little about Governor Reagan, though she had recently received a letter from him about an article she had written for the intellectual magazine *Commentary*. "One day I went to my office at the university," she said later, "and there was a letter from Governor Reagan. It was fairly clear to me that he had written the letter himself—it was not ghostwritten [written by an aide]. He told me he had read this article, and said I had touched a number of themes that interested him. He said he would like to meet me sometime, when he was east or I was west. It was just a nice letter."

She was totally surprised to hear from Reagan. Kirkpatrick said, "I didn't know Ronald Reagan read *Commentary*, I didn't know much about him, and what I did know was not particularly encouraging, from my point of view."

In 1980, Kirkpatrick and Reagan appeared to have little in common. The 54-year-old Kirkpatrick was a distinguished professor of political science at Georgetown University in Washington, D.C., with a long list of publications to her credit—and a lifelong member of the Democratic party. Brought up in small towns in Oklahoma and Illinois, she came from a family of staunch Democrats. When she married Evron Kirkpatrick, a friend of Hubert Humphrey's, she had entered Washington's high-powered Democratic political circles. In 1968, Kirkpatrick and her husband (who is called Kirk) had strongly supported Humphrey when he ran for and narrowly lost the presidency to the Republican candidate, Richard Nixon.

But as the years passed, Kirkpatrick became increasingly dissatisfied with the Democratic party. Her alienation began when the number of those who opposed U.S. support of South Vietnam in that country's war with its Communist neighbor, North Vietnam, grew in the Democratic party. In her opinion, they went too far in attacking American policies and institutions. She deeply believed that the United States must oppose the spread of communism in the world, because Communist governments are very seldom democracies. (Communism generally refers to the system of government and economics based on the ownership of property by the community as a whole. The Soviet Union, for example, has a Communist government. The United States has a democratic government and a capitalist economy, in which individuals or corporations own property.) Kirkpatrick's position on foreign affairs is considered conservative in the spectrum of American political ideas. When George McGovern won the Democratic nomination for president on an antiwar platform in 1972, Kirkpatrick tried to change the party from within, for she profoundly disagreed with his views—decidedly not conservative—about the international activities of the United States. She and other prominent Democrats formed the Coalition for a Democratic Majority (CDM) to wrest control of the party away from McGovern supporters. Members of this coalition—who became known as "neoconservatives" as a result of their foreign policy views—tended to hold liberal positions on domestic issues. For example, some of them encouraged the ratification of the Equal Rights Amendment, many promoted civil rights, and others supported a woman's right to abortion. Nevertheless, they firmly rejected the foreign policy views of most Democrats as being too weak on communism.

In 1976, when one of Kirkpatrick's neoconservative colleagues—Senator Henry "Scoop" Jackson of Washington State—tried to win the Democratic nomination for president, she supported him, but he lost to Jimmy Carter

Despite the support of the CDM, Senator Henry "Scoop" Jackson lost the 1976 Democratic presidential nomination to Jimmy Carter.

in several important primary elections. Kirkpatrick and other members of the CDM were successful in their attempt to add a human rights plank to the platform of the Democratic party but failed to secure a place for Jackson on the Democratic ticket, as either a presidential or vice-presidential nominee.

Recognizing that Jimmy Carter would probably get the nomination, she did not attend the Democratic convention that year, even though she had served on a party committee that helped prepare for the event. She said later, "The outcome was clear." In the November election, she quietly cast her vote for

15

The 1972 presidential campaign of George McGovern (waving) was a turning point in Kirkpatrick's political orientation. Together with other Democrats dissatisfied with the state of the party, she joined the Coalition for a Democratic Majority (CDM) in the first half of the 1970s.

the Republican candidate, Gerald R. Ford.

After Carter was elected, Kirkpatrick was sharply critical of his foreign policies. She published the *Commentary* article that drew Reagan's attention, writing, "The failure of the Carter administration's foreign policy is now clear to everyone except its architects." She warned of the "dramatic Soviet military build-up, matched by the stagnation of American armed forces" and criticized Carter for his policies toward both Iran and Nicaragua, where anti-Communist governments friendly to

the United States had been overthrown by unfriendly governments.

Shortly before Allen telephoned her, Kirkpatrick and other neoconservatives had met with President Carter, at his suggestion, to discuss foreign policy issues. But "he didn't listen," Kirkpatrick told an interviewer from *Vogue*. By the time she answered the phone on that April day, Kirkpatrick's disenchantment with Democrats had been growing for more than 10 years.

Shortly after Kirkpatrick told Allen that she would meet with Reagan, the White House telephoned her. President

Carter wanted her to represent the CDM in foreign policy discussions that the Democratic party was holding. Kirkpatrick told the White House that she was sorry to decline, but she already had a date. "When I hung up," she said later, "I felt I had crossed one of the Rubicons in my life. It was a Rubicon I took a long time to cross." ("Crossing the Rubicon" refers to an act or decision that obligates a person to an irrevocable change. It derives from Julius Caesar's decision to cross the Rubicon River in defiance of the Roman senate.) Although Kirkpatrick was to become one of Reagan's most trusted advisers, it would be several more years before she crossed the Rubicon to become a member of the Republican party.

When she met with Reagan in 1980, Kirkpatrick signed on as a member of his foreign policy advisory group, working closely with Allen. She helped prepare Reagan for the televised debates he had with Carter during the campaign by briefing him on foreign policy issues. Shortly after he was elected, Reagan telephoned Kirkpatrick in Miami, Florida, where she was addressing a university audience. Kirkpatrick remembered that call in an interview with the *Ladies Home Journal*. She said that after her speech, "Kirk and I were having a long, leisurely dinner, just the two of us. When we came back to our hotel room there was a message to call Ronald Reagan. I asked how he was, and he said, 'I'll be better if you agree to be our ambassador to the United Nations.' "

Kirkpatrick accepted Reagan's request, and her appointment to the United Nations (UN), the international peacekeeping organization, was unanimously confirmed by the Senate, where Republicans were in the majority. She gracefully fielded questions from reporters about her party affiliation, telling one writer for the *New York Times*, "I am a Democrat because I have been a Democrat all my life. But that doesn't mean that I always agree with my party."

Kirkpatrick firmly believed that Reagan's election as president—as well as the election of a new Republican majority in the Senate—was a turning point in American politics. She opined, "The elections of 1980 marked the end of a national identity crisis through which the United States had been passing for some ten or fifteen years. This was a period of great national self-doubt and self-denigration for Americans. Now there is a new national consensus in both our domestic and our foreign affairs, and that new consensus reflects a return of the nation's self-confidence."

Reagan's election certainly marked a turning point for Kirkpatrick, whose appointment as the country's first woman ambassador to the UN put her in the international spotlight. She became one of the architects of Reagan's foreign policy, and her *Commentary* article, known as the "Kirkpatrick Doctrine," became the intellectual underpinning of those policies. The Kirkpatrick Doctrine held that authoritarian governments that were friendly

President Jimmy Carter and his family walk down Pennsylvania Avenue in the inaugural parade on January 20, 1977. Kirkpatrick profoundly disagreed with the Carter administration's foreign policy.

to the United States—even though they might be repressive to their citizens—ought to be supported. Totalitarian governments that were unfriendly to the United States should not be supported, she argued. (Authoritarian states are those that concentrate nearly unlimited political power in the hands of one leader; totalitarian states are those that exert total control over their citizens' political, economic, and social life and violently suppress all criticism.) Kirkpatrick believed that authoritarian governments were more likely to develop into democracies than were totalitarian governments. At the UN, and as one of Reagan's closest advisers, she had the opportunity to put her views into action.

As a professor, Kirkpatrick had studied and written about Latin American politics. Now she used her knowledge to influence Reagan's controversial policies toward Nicaragua, a small country in Central America. A civil war broke out there in 1979 in response to the oppressive tactics of President Anastasio Somoza-Debayle, the last in a wealthy family that had dominated Nicaraguan government since 1937. Despite appeals from the United States and other Central American nations to relinquish power, Somoza-Debayle refused and instead ordered massive bombing raids on Nicaraguan civilian areas he suspected held the rebels, known as Sandinistas. The horrified populace increased their support of the Sandinistas. Seven weeks after the revolution began, Somoza fled the country and the victorious Sandinistas took control of the government in July 1979. They nationalized much of the land and half the industries, which gained them substantial initial support from the populace but angered business leaders, who called them Communists and appealed to the United States for help. A group called the contras, which included some former Somoza supporters, opposed the new government, and Reagan subsidized these rebels with shipments of arms and financial help in an effort to prevent the spread of communism, even though many Americans opposed such aid. In 1981, Reagan cut off all U.S. aid to the elected Sandinista government after he accused them of supplying arms to rebels in neighboring El Salvador. With Kirkpatrick's support as a member of the National Security Planning Group (an advisory group to the president), the United States then increased its aid to the Nicaraguan contras. Her careful study and analysis and her newly won position of influence enabled her to put her convictions into action.

At the UN, where vehement criticism of the United States had become a favorite pastime of many small countries, Kirkpatrick worked hard to improve U.S. relations and influence. For example, Cuba and other small countries had repeatedly attacked the United States for what they called its "colonial" and "imperialist" domination of Puerto Rico, a U.S. territory, although free elections had been held in Puerto Rico since 1952 and Puerto Rican citizens had voted against independence from the United States. Kirkpatrick saw Cuba's attacks as U.S. bashing, and she exerted great effort to end them. She also repeatedly spoke out against Soviet expansion. (Before the ascendancy of Mikhail Gorbachev, the foreign policy of the Soviet Union was very different and much more threatening to neighboring nations and capitalist, democratic governments.) "The Soviets had been mounting an extremely aggressive, long-term campaign to transform the UN into a useful political tool for their own purposes of expansion," she said later. Deploring the December 1979 Soviet invasion of Afghanistan, one of its neighbors to the south, Kirkpatrick spoke forcefully to the UN General Assembly, saying, "The invasion was a grave violation of the United Nations Charter.... [It] shook the very foundations of world order."

Kirkpatrick was widely praised by both Democrats and Republicans for her strong stance at the UN. For one of her diplomatic achievements, Reagan called her a "heroine." But she also drew criticism, sometimes because of her sex. She was the only woman ambassador at the UN and the only woman at the highest level of foreign policy circles in the Reagan administration. There had never been a woman who headed a UN delegation of a major country. "I was a very big shock to the foreign policy community," she noted later. "I think I was a very unwelcome shock." Although during her tenure as ambassador she tended to minimize the importance of sexism—saying that any woman in a nontraditional role

encountered it—she did complain when one of her colleagues said she was too temperamental to hold higher office. Kirkpatrick claimed the comment was a classic sexist charge—it was hardly ever directed at men, no matter how much passion they displayed. She also faced the insult of being addressed as "Mrs." instead of "Doctor," for although men with doctoral degrees were routinely addressed as "Doctor," few who spoke to or of Kirkpatrick bothered to recognize her Ph.D. She developed the ability to ignore such discrimination, however, by putting it in perspective. "I go and read a good book, listen to some Bach, absorb myself in music," she told a reporter from *Newsweek*.

Kirkpatrick was also an outsider as a Democrat in a Republican administration. Again, however, she downplayed the importance of party labels, saying her work at the UN was nonpartisan—transcending party lines. She would wait a while longer before crossing that Rubicon.

When Reagan ran for a second term in 1984—this time against the Democratic slate of Walter F. Mondale and Geraldine Ferraro—Kirkpatrick again supported the Republican candidates, despite her formal party affiliation. At the Republican convention in Dallas, she spoke on Reagan's behalf, and her remarks were met with resounding applause. "I thought about it a lot," she said later to a reporter from *Time*. "That was different from anything I had done. That was a real plunge into the very citadel of partisan politics."

Jeane and Evron Kirkpatrick pose in Saint-Rémy-de-Provence, where they spend many summers. The rest of the year they live in Bethesda, Maryland. They have learned to accommodate each other's busy schedules and varied commitments throughout their marriage.

Kirkpatrick visits a local market in Kinshasa, Zaire, with members of the Zairian women's movement. Her post at the UN involved travel all over the world, and her prestigious role in U.S. foreign policy provided inspiration to women of many nations.

But she remained true to her convictions. "It was important that he be reelected," she said. "The alternative was dangerous."

During the convention, at a meeting with editors from *Time*, Kirkpatrick expressed sympathy for Geraldine Ferraro as the first woman vice-presidential candidate. Acknowledging that political opportunities for women were increasing, Kirkpatrick added, "It is a very harsh game, and I do not think women want whatever is at the end of that particular rainbow badly enough to pursue it."

Kirkpatrick soon decided to change her own pursuits. On April 1, 1985, she resigned her post at the UN after serving more than four years, longer than any ambassador in recent history. Later, she commented on her departure date; it was the same day that Allen had telephoned her five years earlier about meeting with Reagan. "April

22

Fools' Day is the significant day in my relationship with the Reagan administration," she said, "and I'm still not sure who the joke was on."

She had achieved her basic goal—beginning to restore American influence at the UN—and now wanted to return to writing and teaching. "It's a very hard life," she said of her years at the UN. "I worked harder than I have ever worked in my life—90 and 100 hour weeks on a regular basis. I didn't have a private life." Kirkpatrick's husband had remained at their home in Bethesda, Maryland, a suburb of Wash-

ington, when she accepted the UN post in New York, and now she rejoined him. She remained, however, a public figure who drew world attention.

Shortly after she resigned from the UN, Kirkpatrick crossed a second Rubicon, to become a registered member of the Republican party. Just as she had waited a long time to leave Democratic politics and work for a Republican administration, she had taken several years to change her party membership. A widely circulated story about one of Kirkpatrick's children indicated how important the Democratic party had

Kirkpatrick's son Douglas (left) humorously recounted how, as a child, he once announced that just as other families might be Quaker or Jewish, his family was Democratic. Kirkpatrick's switch to the Republican party was all the more surprising because of her formerly staunch support of Democrats.

*To Jeane —
who does it all so well —*

Geo Bush

President George Bush, who was U.S. ambassador to the UN from 1971 to 1973, chats with Kirkpatrick in the White House. Kirkpatrick continues to express her influential opinions and analyses of foreign events in her syndicated newspaper column, in televised interviews and roundtable discussions, and on several governmental advisory boards.

been in her life. Young Douglas Kirkpatrick returned home from school and announced to his parents that he and his friends had been discussing "what we are." His parents asked what he meant. Douglas explained that one friend had said he was a Catholic, another that she was a Jew, and another a Quaker—and he had said his family were Democrats. In the Kirkpatrick family, the Democratic party had once held the status of religion.

On April 3, 1985, the Republican party in Washington threw a party to welcome Kirkpatrick to their ranks, having sent out invitations that featured the Republican symbol—an elephant—dancing. During the party George Bush, the vice-president of the United States and then the chairman of the Republican National Committee, joined others in welcoming the newly Republican Kirkpatrick. Bush read a letter from Reagan in which Reagan recalled his own switch from the Democratic to Republican party. In the months that followed, Kirkpatrick's name was repeatedly mentioned as a presidential or vice-presidential candidate for the Republican party in 1988, despite her frequent refusals to run. She had never run for public office and preferred the life of a scholar.

In a 1985 article in *Glamour* magazine, entitled "Why I Think More Women Are Needed at the Pinnacle of World Politics," Kirkpatrick criticized both Democrats and Republicans for their sexism. "I think sexism is alive in the U.S. government; it's alive in American politics. It's alive at the United Nations; it's bipartisan," she wrote. She said she had been accused of being "confrontational" at the UN. "I now think that being tagged as 'confrontational' and being a woman in a high position are very closely related," she wrote. "At a certain level of office, the very fact of a woman's occupancy poses a confrontation with conventional expectations."

Kirkpatrick left high-level office, but she continues her outspoken ways. In 1985 she began writing a column on international politics for the Los Angeles Times syndicate of newspapers. In 1990, her political views continue to be heard throughout the world.

Jeane J. Kirkpatrick, who began life in the staunchly Democratic Jordan family in Oklahoma, had crossed more than one Rubicon to reach the pinnacle of international power. Although she once said, "I've never had a career goal in my life. . . . I guess you could say I'm an experience collector," she had succeeded in many ways. The small-town Democrat had not only become a registered Republican but also a professor, mother, writer, columnist, and the first woman U.S. ambassador to the UN.

Jeane Jordan poses for a picture on her fifth birthday. She showed her interest in books at an early age and had learned to read by the time she was four.

T W O

Small-Town Girl

Jeane Duane Jordan was born on November 19, 1926, in the small town of Duncan, Oklahoma. Located 40 miles from the Texas border, in the southwestern part of the state, Duncan was home to about 3,000 people at the time. Jeane's parents, Welcher F. Jordan and Leona Jordan (née Kile), had moved there from their native Texas. Oklahoma was young in 1926, having been a state for less than 20 years, and its politics were tumultuous. Two governors were impeached for incompetency during the 1920s, and the Ku Klux Klan openly terrorized black people and Catholics in the area.

In several ways, when Jeane was born, Duncan was still a pioneer town. White people had settled there during the early part of the century, on land that had once belonged to the Kiowa, Comanche, and Chickasaw Indians. The town continued to have a large Indian population, and young Jeane grew up hearing the sounds of Indian speech, her only exposure to foreign languages for many years.

Jeane's father worked in the oil industry, which thrived in Oklahoma, especially in Duncan, where an oil boom had begun in 1921. As a drilling contractor, Welcher Jordan drilled oil wells for wildcatters—those sometimes less than prudent speculators who specialize in experimental wells—and Jeane's mother kept his financial records. Jeane was their first, and only, child until her brother Jerry was born when she was eight.

Jeane's mother, an avid reader, nurtured her daughter's love of writing and books. By the time she was four, Jeane knew how to read, and as a second-grader, she proudly wrote her first essay. At 10, she saved enough money from her 50-cent allowance to buy her-

Leona and Welcher Jordan decked Jeane out in a crocheted dress and booties for this photograph, taken in 1927. The Jordans were proud of their daughter, who was their only child until they had a son in 1935.

self a treasured thesaurus, a rather unusual purchase for a young girl and one that pointed out her passion for learning.

The Jordan family was also deeply concerned with civic affairs. Welcher Jordan's father was a Texas justice of the peace—an officer who administers the law on minor offenses and performs marriages—and Jeane watched with fascination as her grandfather carried out his duties and consulted his Texas law books. Like the rest of her family, and most Oklahomans, he was an ardent supporter of Franklin Delano Roosevelt, the Democratic president who served from 1933 to 1945 and guided the nation through the economic depression of the 1930s and World War II.

Jeane also listened with fascination to family stories about the Civil War, which raged from 1861 to 1865. Although the fighting ended about 60 years before Jeane was born, men of her grandfathers' generation had participated in it, and families told and retold tales of the bloody conflict. The war had severed the Northern (Yankee) and Southern (Rebel) parts of the nation over the issue of slavery. The two sides of her own family had taken different stands during the war: Her father's grandfather fought with the Southern Confederacy, or proslavery, side, and her mother's grandfather was an officer with the Northern Union, or antislavery, forces. Although Oklahoma had not been a state during the Civil War, many of its inhabitants—including the Chickasaw Indians—had fought with the Confederate forces. To the young Jeane, Oklahoma seemed to be a Confederate state, and her sympathies lay with that side.

But Jeane's ideas about the Civil War soon changed. In 1938, when she was 12, she and her family moved north to

Illinois, where an oil boom was occurring in the southern part of the state. The Jordans settled at first in Vandalia. Like Duncan, Vandalia was a small town, but its history and politics presented a sharp contrast to Jeane's old home. The young girl felt as if she had moved to the Yankee North.

Illinois had not only been a Union state but also was the home state of Abraham Lincoln, often called the Great Emancipator, who freed the slaves when he served as president during the Civil War. Everywhere in Vandalia, reminders of Civil War history

popped up. Jeane learned that this was where Lincoln had served in the state legislature before he became president. She heard the story of the "Long-Nine"—the group of six-foot-tall legislators that Lincoln organized to move the state capital to Springfield. The junior high she attended had been a stop on the Underground Railroad, the secret system developed by antislavery advocates and former slaves for hiding escaped slaves and helping them flee to freedom in Canada. Jeane's eighth-grade history teacher, Miss Elam, was particularly good at making the Civil

Jeane romps in the family driveway on her first birthday. As she grew older, she listened with fascination to family stories about the Civil War. Two of her great-grandfathers had served in that war, although they fought on different sides.

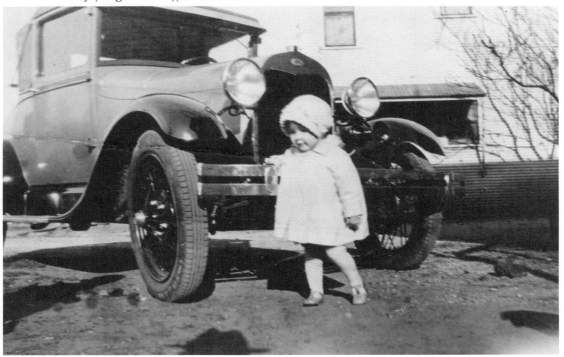

29

Jeane's lifelong passion for the works of Johann Sebastian Bach began in high school. An accomplished piano student, she recalled that learning to play his études "was the first time I understood what music was about."

War come alive for her students, and Jeane soon became an ardent fan of President Lincoln. Years later, a bust of Lincoln would grace her office in Washington.

Jeane's family changed more than their address when they moved to Vandalia; they also changed churches. There had been only two churches (both Protestant) in Duncan—Methodist and Southern Baptist—and Jeane's family had been Southern Baptist, a rather strict denomination. Vandalia presented a wider range to choose from, and Jeane's mother picked a more liberal church, the Northern Baptist, which the family attended every Sunday.

At the same time Jeane was finding her way around Vandalia and learning the history of the Civil War, another war was beginning in Europe. Throughout the 1930s, Adolf Hitler, the fanatically anti-Semitic leader of Germany's Nazi (National Socialist) party, steadily gained power. On September 1, 1939, when Jeane was 13, Hitler invaded western Poland and started World War II. Two weeks later, acting according to a pact with Hitler, the Soviet Union seized the eastern sections of Poland. Soon, Japan, Italy, and Germany formed the Axis powers and waged war against the United States, Great Britain, France, and eventually the Soviet Union. The fighting spread over Europe, northern Africa, the South Pacific islands, and the Atlantic and Pacific oceans. By the time the war was over, 61 of the world's 67 countries had entered the war, and 50 million people had died. The number of dead encompassed not only casualties of war but also civilians, including 6 million Poles, half of them Jews who perished in Nazi death camps, victims of Hitler's bizarre theories and virulent anti-Semitism. By the end of the war, Hitler would kill 6 million European Jews. While Jeane was aware of the invasion of Poland, like most Americans, she did not feel directly affected by the war until two years later, when the U.S. naval base at Pearl Harbor in Hawaii was attacked by the Japanese.

After two years in Vandalia, the Jordan family moved again, to Mount Vernon, Illinois, some 60 miles south of Vandalia. Although Jeane had liked Vandalia, her mother was dissatisfied with the community. She thought the schools in Mount Vernon would be better for Jeane and her brother. A town of about 12,000 people, Mount Vernon had been settled by southerners, and it retained its southern charm.

In Mount Vernon, Jeane's passion for literature and music blossomed. She discovered Shakespeare's plays, reading *The Tragedy of Julius Caesar* for a class during her sophomore year. "I was enormously struck by it," she said later, "and I bought myself the complete works of Shakespeare. I read most of them—the histories and tragedies especially—but I kept this a secret because this was not part of life for a normal girl, and I wanted to lead a normal life." She had taken piano lessons in Duncan and Vandalia, and now, under her teacher Mabel Tavey, she studied and played the études of the 18th-century German composer Johann Sebastian Bach. Years later, Jeane recalled, "I felt that was the first time I understood what music was about."

Jeane was an outstanding student, making straight A's, and she edited the high school newspaper and acted in plays. For her senior paper, she wrote an essay on four novels by George Eliot, a British woman writer of the 19th century. Eliot, whose real name was Mary Ann Evans, wrote under a male pseudonym because of prejudice against women writers.

Like Eliot, Jeane, too, was experiencing prejudice against women. Her brother Jerry was allowed to take summer jobs working in the oil fields. Jeane, however, had to spend her summers at home, helping her mother, reading, and playing the piano. Her parents, like many in those years, thought it was inappropriate for a young lady to work outside the home. The only job Jeane had until she was 24 years old was to occasionally fill in for the social editor of the Mount Vernon newspaper when the editor went on vacation.

When she was not at home or school, Jeane had an active social life. She had a boyfriend with whom she "went steady," and both enjoyed attending movies. Movies starring actress Katharine Hepburn, who often played independent career women, were Jeane's favorites. As an adult, like her movie idol, Jeane was often noted for her aristocratic bearing and the strong character of her face.

It was during a Sunday afternoon movie that Jeane first learned that the United States had been attacked by the Japanese. On December 7, 1941, the woman who owned the Mount Vernon movie theater interrupted the film to tell the audience that the Japanese had bombed Pearl Harbor. Within days the United States was at war. For the next several years, until the conflict ended in 1945, Jeane was acutely aware of World War II, as were most Americans.

By the time she finished high school, Jeane's lifelong interests in politics, history, writing, literature, and music

were firmly established. After her graduation, she departed for nearby Stephens College, a private two-year women's college in Columbia, Missouri, another small town in the Midwest.

Unlike most colleges, Stephens assisted its students with transportation to the school. Jordan's parents drove her to St. Louis, Missouri, where she met other women headed for Stephens and boarded the Stephens Special, a train bound for Columbia.

Jeane was living in Mount Vernon, Illinois, and attending high school when World War II began. In later years she recalled how she learned of the December 7, 1941, Japanese attack on the U.S. naval base at Pearl Harbor, Hawaii—she was in a movie theater when the show was interrupted by the tragic announcement.

Stephens was founded as the Columbia Female Academy in 1833, offering elementary and high school instruction. The school later became the Columbia Baptist Female College, but by the time Jordan arrived in 1944, it was known as Stephens College and had no religious affiliation. Until the 1960s, when it became a four-year college, Stephens offered a two-year associate of arts degree.

When Jordan attended Stephens, the school had a dual identity—as a finishing school, featuring a golf course, a lake, and riding stables, designed to prepare privileged women for marriage

33

In 1944, Jordan entered Stephens College in Missouri. During her two years there, she allowed her academic interests to blossom by enrolling in a demanding schedule of liberal arts courses and writing for both the school newspaper and the school literary magazine.

and social niceties, and as a women's college with a progressive curriculum. Jordan eschewed most of the finishing-school aspects of Stephens and concentrated on her interests in writing, literature, and history. At home in the college environment, she gave full rein to her intellectual interests without fear of appearing odd. She enrolled in a liberal arts curriculum and pursued numerous extracurricular activities.

Almost immediately, she began working on the school newspaper, *Stephens Life,* and the school literary magazine, the *Stephens Standard.* She discovered authors with whom she was unfamiliar and particularly enjoyed the works of Virginia Woolf, a British writer of such feminist classics as *A Room of One's Own.* Jeane also got involved in the school's religion and philosophy programs.

Although Stephens was not far from Jordan's home in Illinois, she returned home only at Christmas and at the end of the school year. She again took the Stephens Special to St. Louis and was either met by her parents or, if gasoline was scarce, took a bus from St. Louis to Mount Vernon. Gasoline was rationed because of the war, and although Jordan's father had unlimited gas for his work in the oil fields, he was mindful of his civic responsibility and careful not to abuse his privilege.

During the summer between her two years at Stephens, Jordan made her first trip to New York City, riding the train 825 miles east to visit her college roommate Cynthia. With Cynthia and her brother as guides, she saw Staten Island, the Statue of Liberty, the Bowery, and the Brooklyn Bridge. "I walked for a week," she said later. "I was impressed with the size and diversity of it."

Jordan's parents expected her to return home to Mount Vernon after she completed the two-year program at Stephens. Few women in those days pursued higher education, and the Jordans thought their daughter would now live the life of a lady—reading, playing the piano, and helping her mother. But Jordan had other ideas. She took examinations and won a full scholarship to the University of Chicago. At the same time, she applied and gained acceptance to Barnard College, one of the oldest and finest women's colleges in the country, affiliated with Columbia University in New York City.

So eager was Jordan to continue her studies that she decided to start classes at the University of Chicago during the summer after she graduated from Stephens. She planned to study political philosophy, a field that was particularly strong at the university. In June she took the train to Chicago and looked for housing. There was no housing available on campus, but she found a room off campus, far from the university, and tried to enroll. Her registration file, however, had been misplaced, and she spent three days waiting until it was found. By then, most of the classes she wanted to take had been filled. She was becoming exasperated.

The last straw came one evening as she was returning home from the library, tired and with blisters on her feet. She stood waiting for a bus on Michigan Avenue, near the edge of Grant Park, when a threatening gang of men surrounded her and started backing her toward the trees in the park. She was able to break away and hail a taxi but decided then to return home. She would go to Barnard instead of Chicago.

Jordan had been in Chicago for only two weeks when she went back to Mount Vernon. Two days after she got home, she received a postcard from the International House at Chicago, a complex that provided on-campus housing for students, saying they had a room for her. If the card had come a few days earlier, she might have stayed at the University of Chicago. Instead she set off on a different journey.

Jordan's high school portrait was taken in spring 1944. By the time she graduated from Stephens College two years later, she was determined to pursue the life of a scholar and an academic, although very few American women did so at the time. She enrolled at Barnard College, part of Columbia University, in New York City in 1946 in order to earn her baccalaureate degree.

THREE

An Intellectual Education

When Jordan's train arrived in New York City that September 1946, Pennsylvania Station was bustling with crowds. People rushed by, jostling her as she carried two large bags through the huge train station. Finally, she made her way outside, where she took a taxi to Morningside Heights on the northwestern side of the island of Manhattan, to Hewitt Hall at Barnard College.

One of the "Seven Sisters"—seven women's colleges founded in the 1800s, akin to the then all-male Ivy League and, like them, located in the Northeast—Barnard had been in existence for almost 60 years when Jordan arrived there. The college was among the pioneers in making rigorous higher education available to women. Dean Gildersleeve, the woman who headed Barnard, had worked hard to attract students and teachers from all over the world, and the school was renowned for its international population, which

greatly appealed to Jordan. When she arrived, she learned that Dean Gildersleeve had added yet another distinction to her long list of achievements. She had been the only woman delegate representing the United States at the 1945 conference in San Francisco, where the UN was established at the end of World War II.

The name United Nations had sometimes been used during the war to refer to the Allies—those countries that allied themselves against the Axis. During the war, discussions among the Allies regarding a permanent organization to deal with threats to world peace cropped up in 1944 at the Dumbarton Oaks Conference and at the Yalta Conference the following year. After the war, representatives of all the Allied, or United Nations, countries met in San Francisco to sign and ratify the UN charter, forming an organization designed "to save succeeding generations from the scourge of war," as the charter stated. The UN conference was attended by 50 countries but was dominated by the Big Four: the United States, the United Kingdom (Great Britain), the Soviet Union, and China.

In March 1946, just a few months before Jordan arrived at Barnard, the UN held its first meetings in New York City. The UN's Security Council—composed of representatives from the Big Four and France as permanent members and representatives from six other countries as nonpermanent members—had as its primary responsibility the maintenance of international peace and security. Its members met initially on the Hunter College campus in the borough of the Bronx, a section of the city north of Manhattan. The UN's General Assembly—which included representatives from all member countries—needed much larger quarters and met in a building where New York's World's Fair of 1939–40 had been held, in Queens, a borough to the east. A few years later, in 1950, the UN moved to its permanent location in the Turtle Bay section of Manhattan, where an international team of architects had designed a complex of stunning marble-and-glass buildings large enough to hold all the UN's committees and subgroups. This UN area of New York became a separate entity, over which New York City had no jurisdiction, and maintained its own police force and postal service, with its own stamps.

While the UN was holding its first meetings, Jordan was settling into her new surroundings at Barnard. Her early weeks there were intensely lonely, until she got acquainted with the women in her dormitory. One of the first friends she made was a woman who lived across the hall, Anne DeLattre, a student from France, who became her best friend.

The first task Jordan faced was what to study. At Stephens she had studied liberal arts—philosophy, history, and literature—and loved each subject. At Chicago she had planned to study political philosophy. Now, after much soul-searching, she chose political science, reasoning that she could continue studying philosophy and history as a political science major and that she could always pursue literature on her own. Besides, she had practical considerations. "My father was concerned with whether I would ever get a job," she said years later. If she was going to pursue an intellectual education, she decided it ought to be one that would help her get a job someday.

It was an exciting time and place to study political science. The Second World War had ended in 1945, when Germany and Japan surrendered. Now, in 1946, the survivors of Hitler's death camps and others who fled the wreckage of the war were seeking refuge in the United States, and many of them were settling in New York City. One of Jeane's mentors in the political science department was Franz Neumann, a Jew who had escaped Germany and written a book about Hitler's reign. Neumann's book *Behemoth: The Structure and Practice of National Socialism, 1933–1944* examined how

Jordan found the mix of foreign and U.S. students at Barnard thrilling, and life in New York City presented many more opportunities than did life in Mount Vernon. She quickly decided to major in political science, studied European political movements, and made friends with Anne DeLattre, a woman from France.

McGill University is located in Montreal, Canada, in the province of Quebec, where French is widely spoken. The summer Jordan spent there in an intensive French-language program gave her the opportunity to both learn French in the classroom ·and use it in daily conversation.

conditions in Germany had led to Hitler's popularity. Jordan read *Behemoth* and became interested in nondemocratic governments—those governments that do not allow their citizens to take part in the political process or have civil or political rights. For example, nondemocratic governments do not hold free elections, so the people cannot choose their leaders, and such governments often censor the press and

arrest or imprison citizens without a fair trial or defense.

In addition to her political science studies, Jordan discovered a new passion for French. Stephens had not had a language requirement, but Barnard required its students to pass a rigorous language examination before graduation. Jordan had studied Spanish in high school and at Stephens, but her instruction had not been adequate.

When she was told to enroll in a third-year Spanish course at Barnard to prepare herself for the language exam, she did so but did not do well in the subject. "The teacher blasted me in class for my pronunciation, it was so bad," she recalled. Jordan went to the dean and asked to transfer to a beginning French course and then set to work with determination. "I literally memorized my whole French book, to the point that I could not only recite the verbs, but all the examples as well. I really learned that basic French book."

With Anne DeLattre, Jordan spent long hours practicing her French. "She heaped scorn on me when I spoke, as she would put it, 'as though I had a mouthful of mashed potatoes,' but she was very patient. She would go over and over the French sounds with me until I got them right."

Jordan continued studying French the summer after her first year at Barnard, her junior year. She spent her school vacation in Montreal, in the French part of Canada, at McGill University, in an intensive French program, dedicating herself to mastering the language. "I worked very hard," she said years later, "probably more systematically than I have worked on anything in my life." When she returned to Barnard for her senior year, she took the language examination and passed with high marks. The chairman of the French Department was so impressed that he asked her to come see him about pursuing graduate work in French. Jordan was delighted—"it was probably the greatest academic triumph of my life," she noted—but she was not concerned with pursuing a language degree. Although she was fascinated with French literature and politics, she was more interested in the language as a tool, rather than a focus, of study.

Jordan was now thoroughly immersed in intellectual pursuits. At Stephens she had taken part in extracurricular activities, but at Barnard she mainly studied, taking time out occasionally to go to the theater or art museums. Her stated ambition was to be a spinster teacher at a women's college, and her favorite author was the feminist writer Virginia Woolf.

When she received her B.A. degree in the spring of 1948, Jordan skipped Barnard's graduation ceremonies—as she had those at Stephens—and went home to Mount Vernon. She was now highly educated for a woman of her generation. Less than 6 percent of women her age had completed 4 years of college, and less than 23 percent had finished 4 years of high school. But Jordan was not content to stop with an undergraduate degree. The next fall she returned to New York and enrolled in a master's program at Columbia, for an advanced degree in political science.

With Franz Neumann as her adviser, Jordan set about studying the rise of fascism in Britain during the 1930s. Fascism—a nondemocratic system of government in which a dictator rules and promotes belligerent nationalism, or loyalty to one's country at the expense of others—became prevalent in Europe during World War II. Hitler in

Herbert Marcuse, another German refugee, taught at Columbia while Jordan worked on her master's degree there. She found his lectures and books fascinating but difficult.

Germany and Benito Mussolini in Italy were both Fascist leaders; Francisco Franco in Spain was another. Although both Hitler and Mussolini supported the Fascist movement in Britain, many of the British Fascists were arrested and put in prison, and the movement there ended by 1940. Jordan investigated how a Fascist movement could have arisen and occurred at all in Britain, in a democratic context.

While she was working on her master's thesis, Jordan attended several lectures by Herbert Marcuse, another German scholar who had fled Hitler and was now lecturing at Columbia. She read Marcuse's books—one on the German philosopher G. W. F. Hegel and another about the theories of Sigmund Freud, the founder of psychoanalysis. She found Marcuse's work dense and complex, like many German philosophical books. Although they were difficult reading, Jordan thought them fascinating. Like Marcuse, she, too, was concerned with the effects of philosophy and psychology on politics.

Two years after she started graduate school, Jordan completed her master's thesis. She had also earned almost all the credits she needed toward a doctoral degree, lacking only one seminar and a dissertation (a book-length paper). But she could not continue, for she had to look for a job. Her father had grown tired of supporting her and insisted she go to work for a while.

Jordan chose Washington, D.C., the headquarters of the federal government, as the place to put her education to use. Equipped with a letter of introduction from Franz Neumann to two officials at the Department of State (the government agency that deals with foreign policy), she took the train to Washington.

Jean-Paul Sartre poses in St. Mark's Square in Venice on a trip to Italy. Jordan found herself much concerned with Sartre and his writing when she studied in Paris on a fellowship in 1952, for she was in France to explore the topic of communism and its appeal to French intellectuals, and he was one of the leading figures in public debate on the subject.

FOUR

Transitions

The letters of introduction Neumann gave Jordan were addressed to Herbert Marcuse and Evron Kirkpatrick, both high-ranking State Department officials. She was familiar with Marcuse's work from her studies at Columbia but knew less about Kirkpatrick. After meeting the two men, she considered her options and decided the job that Kirkpatrick described, that of a research analyst, sounded more attractive.

A former professor at the University of Minnesota, Kirkpatrick served as a liaison between universities and the State Department. His office brought academic studies on foreign affairs to the government's attention—a task that sounded interesting to Jordan. After spending two years at Columbia among professors and other graduate students, she was ably equipped to help disseminate academic information to those outside the university community. She happily accepted the job Kirkpatrick offered. The choice was fortunate for her in several ways. She could not have known it then, but her path and Marcuse's would diverge greatly in the future. Years later, Marcuse became a prominent philosopher of the New Left, the political theory that buttressed the antiwar movement of the 1960s, toward which she had very little sympathy.

When Jordan began her new—and first—job, she found that her day-to-day duties were much different than she had imagined. Although the office's broad purpose was to gather academic information for the government, her particular tasks were to edit and condense interviews with Soviet refugees.

In the postwar period, reports were just starting to surface about "purges" of millions of Soviet citizens by their

45

Communist leader, Joseph Stalin. Purges—in which victims were swiftly and suddenly arrested and then put to death or sent to prison camps, often without any kind of public or fair trial—were supposedly the means of "purifying" the Communist party of dissident members. Actually, Stalin used them to maintain his personal power and inspire fear in the populace. During Stalin's rule, it is estimated that one Soviet family in two had one of its members in a prison camp. Jordan was given numerous interviews with refugees who had made their way out of the Soviet Union and across war-ravaged Eastern Europe into Germany and then to the United States. Their horrifying accounts of life under Soviet communism made a lasting impression on her. At Columbia, she had studied nondemocratic governments and heard lectures by Neumann and Marcuse, intellectuals who had fled a Fascist regime. Now she read how a nondemocratic, Communist regime affected ordinary people, wrenching their day-to-day lives.

Evron Kirkpatrick occasionally came by Jordan's office and took her to lunch. Although he was 15 years her senior, the experienced official and the recent graduate greatly enjoyed talking about politics. Kirkpatrick was much nearer the center of political life in the capital than Jordan was at that point. In his previous position at the University of Minnesota, Kirkpatrick had taught government to Hubert H. Humphrey and helped manage Humphrey's successful campaign for mayor of Minneapolis in 1945. By the time Jordan arrived in the capital, Humphrey was a senator from Minnesota, living in Washington, and had maintained his friendship with Kirkpatrick.

Jordan was enjoying her life in Washington, where she had several friends from Columbia, but she soon grew bored with the bureaucracy at the State Department. When she saw a notice in the *New York Times* about a fellowship sponsored by the French government, she decided to apply. With the French fellowship, she reasoned, she could resume her doctoral work and also perfect her French-language skills. Happily, she won the fellowship, to study at the Institute de Science Politique (Institute of Political Science) of the University of Paris.

After a year at the State Department, Jordan left Washington in September 1952 and sailed for France. She traveled third-class on the *Ile de France*, one of France's great ocean liners, named for the region in France where Paris is located. During World War II, the *Ile de France* had been used by the Allies to transport nearly half a million troops and support staff across the Atlantic. After the war, when it was refitted for civilian use, the *Ile de France* was the fifth-largest ship in the world. Jordan enjoyed the trip and eagerly looked forward to arriving in France.

Jordan was excited to finally see Paris, the capital of France, a city she had read about for years. Paris was still recovering from the war at that point, particularly from the effects of the Nazi invasion and occupation, which began in 1940. As the Germans marched toward Paris and flooded into the city, more than half the Parisian population had fled to the south of France, where a new French government, called the Vichy government, which collaborated with the Germans, was established. That same year, General Charles de Gaulle, leader of the French Resistance (a group of men and women who secretly worked against the occupying German forces), set up the Free French government in London, England. The Vichy officials collaborated with the Germans until the invaders occupied all of France in 1942. Not until 1944, when the Allies liberated Paris and de Gaulle returned, set up a provisional government, and purged the government of Vichy collaborators, did the city begin returning to normal. A huge infusion of U.S. aid also helped the French begin to rebuild their war-torn economy. Six years later, in 1952, Paris was coming back to life as its intellectual and cultural vitality returned.

Jordan settled into Reid Hall, then an international residence for women, which had been established by a Barnard alumna. "It had one great advantage," she said years later. "It was

A 1931 photograph shows Joseph Stalin around the time his vicious purges of the Soviet Union's Communist party became particularly bloody. Jordan's first job, as a research analyst for the Department of State, involved editing interviews with Soviet citizens who had fled from Stalin's autocratic rule.

A 1944 photograph of Isigny, France, reveals the devastation World War II wreaked on parts of the country. (The poster on the right warns that looting is punishable by death.) France had begun to rebuild by the time Jordan traveled there, but economic conditions had not completely returned to normal, leading to impassioned political arguments among French citizens.

warm and had endless hot water." Because Paris was suffering postwar shortages of fuel and many of the city's utilities and buildings had been severely damaged or destroyed, heat and hot water were welcome—and rather rare—amenities.

Jordan soon decided, however, to forgo the warmth and comfort of Reid Hall. "It became clear to me that I was not really going to practice my French or learn how the French people lived, if I stayed there," she said later. She looked at the *International Herald Tribune*, an English-language newspaper, and studied the advertisements for rented accommodations. Soon she found a room in the apartment of a French widow, on the rue de Lubeck, near the place du Trocadero. She prepared to plunge into the daily routine of a Parisian student, shopping in the open-air markets, studying in the library, sipping coffee in cafés, and discussing the latest trends and thought in politics, philosophy, and literature. (By coincidence, a few years after Jordan's stay there, the UN established an important agency just a few miles from where she lived. American, Italian, and French architects designed a building to house the United Nations Educational, Scientific and Cultural Organization—or UNESCO—an agency dedicated to the exchange of information among nations.)

In her new home, heat and hot water were scarce, but Jordan was happy to be in a real French environment. She attended classes at the University of Paris and began to pursue her work at the Bibliothèque Nationale, one of the world's great libraries. Before leaving New York, she had met with her mentor, Franz Neumann, and planned her doctoral research. She would write on a contemporary subject: the appeal of communism to French intellectuals and professionals.

Sidewalk cafés and bistros (small, informal restaurants) were filled with the clamor of political conversation then. French citizens had much to think and argue about. France's economy had been ruined by the German occupation, and the provisional government that ruled from 1944 to 1946 had been determined to create a new social system, devoted to the ideals of personal liberty and basic economic equality. As part of their effort, they instituted a system of social welfare by which what remained of France's financial industry and utilities were nationalized (owned and run by the government). France's damaged economy was hard put to support such a program, however, and inflation raged despite the economic assistance program of the United States, called the Marshall Plan. Food was scarce and expensive, and observers estimated that up to 80 percent of a worker's wages went to pay for it. Tempers ran high and loyalties were fierce among French men and women struggling to rebuild their nation under such trying circumstances.

After de Gaulle's provisional government disbanded at the end of the war, and the Fourth Republic, a reorganized French government, was formed in 1946, a variety of political parties tried to take control of the legislature and implement their own plans and methods of restoring France. Among them were the Communists, who were accepted as a regular political party and found much support among the workers. Other strong political parties formed, including one composed of supporters of de Gaulle, who were among those most vehemently opposed to communism. Kirkpatrick had chosen a lively topic to research.

Working men and women were not the only supporters of the Communists. By 1952, many prominent French intellectuals were aligning themselves with the Communist party or holding public debates about why they would not. Two of these thinkers, Jean-Paul Sartre and Albert Camus, particularly interested Jordan. Both men had served in the French Resistance, secretly fighting Hitler's rule, and Sartre had been captured by the Germans and spent several months in a prisoner-of-war camp. During the war, both Camus and

Despite a serious illness that was not correctly diagnosed for months, Jordan kept up a busy schedule of study and traveled when she could. She took an especially enjoyable trip to Bordeaux, the center of one of France's most well known wine-producing regions.

room, Jordan's health began to deteriorate. She had been ill with respiratory infections in Washington but thought she had recovered. Now, in her cold Paris room, the infections and fever returned. She went to a doctor and was admitted to the American hospital. There one doctor told her she might have leukemia; another claimed that she might have Hodgkin's disease—

both terminal illnesses. Eventually, after leaving the hospital and suffering from colds throughout the winter, her symptoms were diagnosed in the spring. A brilliant French research physician, Professor Mallarmé, who was referred to as "a professor of blood," told Jordan that she had rheumatic fever. "I developed a lot of respect for French medicine," she said later. Once she was diagnosed and treated for rheumatic fever, her symptoms disappeared. Her health would not fully return, however, for another two or three years.

Despite her illness, Jordan found time to enjoy Paris and travel outside the city. On one memorable trip, she took the train to Bordeaux, a city on the Atlantic coast famous for its vineyards and its 18th-century architecture. Her lifelong love affair with France had begun.

While she was in Paris, Jordan kept up with politics in the United States and made her first contribution to a political campaign. In 1952, Adlai E. Stevenson, a Democrat from her home state of Illinois, ran for president against Dwight D. Eisenhower. Jordan used her small stipend from the French government to send a check to the Stevenson campaign. Stevenson lost his bid for the presidency, but several years later, when John F. Kennedy was president, he would serve as U.S. ambassador to the UN, the post Jordan herself would eventually hold.

Near the end of her stay in Paris, Jordan picked up a copy of the *International Herald Tribune*, for she liked to keep abreast of world events. That day's copy bore bad news. To her shock and horror, she read that Franz Neumann had died in a car accident in the Alps. Her adviser and mentor, who had guided her studies and encouraged her intellectual development, had been tragically killed. Neumann had survived Hitler's concentration camps and incisively investigated the rise of fascism. His abiding concern with the evils of that particular political system had helped inspire Jordan's own interest in nondemocratic governments, but now she realized she would have to continue to explore the subject on her own. Dismayed, Jordan prepared to return to New York, uncertain what she would do next but steadfast in her determination to study nondemocratic politics, or totalitarianism—what she would later refer to as "the harm that governments can do."

Shortly before she returned to the United States, Jordan's friend from the State Department, Evron Kirkpatrick, arrived in Paris on a business trip. He telephoned her and took her out to dinner several times; they again enjoyed long, spirited conversations about politics. Before he left Paris and went on to England, they briefly discussed their travel plans for returning to the United States. Neither one was sure which ship would take them home. As it turned out, however, Kirkpatrick was on Jordan's ship. During the Atlantic crossing, the two had dinner together every evening.

Back in the United States, Jordan went to the chairman of the political science department at Columbia and asked what she should do. She needed a new doctoral adviser. The chairman said he was sorry, but no one on the faculty was interested in contemporary French politics. She would have to change her topic or wait until Columbia hired another professor who was interested in French politics. Chagrined and disappointed because she had just spent 10 months working on her dissertation, Jordan decided to postpone her graduate work.

After a trip home to Mount Vernon, she returned to Washington but decided against going back to work at the State Department. She found a job at the Economic Cooperation Administration, assisting the director, Harry Price, who was writing a book on the Marshall Plan—the U.S. economic initiative that helped Europe rebuild itself after the war.

In her work with Price, Jordan was angered by a blatant expression of sexism. She wrote several chapters of his book, those that dealt with the political aspects of the Marshall Plan, but when the book *The Marshall Plan and Its Meaning* was published, Price did not even acknowledge her contribution. Irritated but undaunted, she set to work looking for a new job.

Jeane and Evron Kirkpatrick cut their wedding cake on February 20, 1955, in the Jordans' Mount Vernon home. She was 28; he was 43. The two spent their honeymoon outside Chicago, at a political science convention.

FIVE

Beginning a Career

Jordan's determination paid off once again, and at last she found rewarding employment. She accepted a new position as a research associate at George Washington University, and it became the first job she found truly satisfying. There, in the Human Resources Research Office, she worked on a research project funded by the Defense Department. It involved studying the experience of Chinese prisoners of war whom the United States had captured during the recent Korean War.

The war in Korea lasted from 1951 to 1953 and had its roots in the postwar conflict between the United States and the Soviet Union as well as in Korea's tumultuous history. Japan had annexed Korea in 1910 and subjected Koreans to great political and cultural oppression. Despite the efforts of Korean nationalists (who were often at a disadvantage because of their factional differences),

Japanese control lasted until the end of World War II, when Japan was defeated and forced to surrender its colonies. Various Korean factions sought help from larger powers to organize their new nation. The Soviet Union supervised the surrender of the Japanese north of the 38th parallel (a line of latitude), and the United States oversaw the Japanese surrender south of that line. North Korea, where Communist support was strong, gravitated toward the Soviets. South Korea turned to the United States.

Efforts to make the newly freed peninsula into one nation were unsuccessful, mainly as a result of Soviet insistence on maintaining a Communist North. Although the UN attempted to supervise free elections throughout all of Korea, the Soviets refused to allow UN observers or UN-supervised elections in the North. They

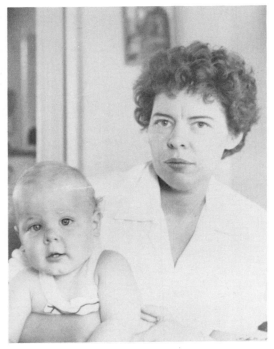

Kirkpatrick sits with her son Stuart in 1960. She did not work full-time while raising her children but had no intention of abandoning scholarship. Instead, she found part-time freelance research work. Referring to motherhood and an academic career, she later noted, "My motto is 'refuse to choose.' "

aided the North Koreans in setting up a government and then withdrew their military forces in 1949; the United States did the same for South Korea. North Korea was firmly Communist; South Korea was not. In June 1950, the North Korean army invaded South Korea, and the UN called on member nations to help South Korea repel the invaders. The United States and Great Britain sent into combat troops that helped South Korea force the North Koreans out of the territory they had overrun, until China, which had become Communist in 1949, sent forces of its own to aid North Korea. Battles raged back and forth around the 38th parallel, and neither side made substantial gains, although the cost in lives was high. Talks regarding the end of hostilities had begun as early as 1951, but no conclusion could be reached because the Communists insisted that all prisoners of war from their side be returned to them—by force if necessary. Two years later, they finally agreed to a truce that included a provision for a neutral commission to screen prisoners who begged not to be returned. Jordan's job involved examining the interviews of the Chinese prisoners who were refusing to go back to their country after the war, in 1954.

Jordan read in-depth interviews with these Chinese prisoners of war. Why did they not want to return to Communist China? What had happened to them during the Communist revolution in China? Jordan found their answers horrifying. They reminded her of the accounts by refugees from Stalin's Communist regime. Again she saw the impact on individual lives of a totalitarian government.

Between 1948 and 1952, Mao Zedong, the leader of the Chinese Communist revolution, had instituted "rectification" programs to reeducate Chinese citizens in Communist doctrine, using harsh techniques that many observers called thought control. The Chinese rectification programs were not as bloody as Stalin's purges in the Soviet Union in the 1930s, but their aim was similar to Stalin's purges: ensuring the strictest adherence to Communist doctrine and total loyalty to one supreme leader.

Jordan was deeply interested in the substance of this research but found the investigative methods used at George Washington University fascinating as well. For the first time, she worked with an interdisciplinary team of social scientists—including a sociologist, a psychologist, and a social psychologist. At Columbia she had received a traditional education in political science, philosophy, and history. At George Washington University she learned the techniques of the social sciences, such as how to design and conduct an effective poll to elicit accurate information from people about their views. Years later, she would use this knowledge repeatedly in polls she designed and conducted for the Democratic party. She continued to encounter and make use of the interdisciplinary approach to research throughout her career.

When she was not working, Jordan was still dating Evron Kirkpatrick, who had left the State Department and become the executive director of the American Political Science Association. In 1955, after dating for four years, they decided to marry. They traveled to Jordan's parents' home in Mount Vernon and on February 20 were married in her parents' living room.

At her small, simple wedding, Jordan wore a cocktail-length gown of muted aqua lace, designed by Oleg Cassini, which she later said she could afford only because a friend's father manufactured them. The Baptist minister from her parents' church officiated. Jeane Duane Jordan took her husband's surname, as almost all women did then, and became Jeane Jordan Kirkpatrick. She was 28 years old; her husband was 43 years old. If her parents had any misgivings about the age difference, they did not express them. "My father was greatly relieved that I had gotten married at all," Kirkpatrick said years later. "He would have liked me to marry earlier, when I was 22, 23, or 24." But Kirkpatrick was self-confidently setting her own timetable, and after the ceremony, she and her new husband departed for an unusual honeymoon.

The Kirkpatricks celebrated their honeymoon at a political science convention at Northwestern University, in a suburb of Chicago. Years later, when questioned about this location, neither of them found their choice odd. They were intellectuals. A political science convention was a fine place to enjoy the first days of their marriage.

When they returned to Washington, Kirkpatrick and her husband settled into their home in the Georgetown section of the city. She continued working at George Washington until her first child, Douglas, was born on July 17, 1956. During her pregnancy she had planned to return to work a little while after the baby was born.

Within 24 hours of Douglas's birth, she decided not to do so. "I was hit very hard by the stirrings of motherhood," she later told an interviewer from *Vogue* magazine. "I had mixed feelings about getting married, getting pregnant; and then suddenly here was this incredible creature, and it was like being infatuated but it doesn't end." Kirkpatrick resigned her job at George Washington and began working as a mother. For the next several years, she was a part-time mother and part-time scholar. Years later, she told a journalist from *Working Woman*, "I think any woman who voluntarily deals herself out of motherhood is making a terrible mistake." At the same time, she added, "If a woman declines to develop her intellectual, aesthetic or professional skills, she also is dealing herself out of major life experiences. Why should anybody voluntarily truncate her life in such a fashion? My motto is 'refuse to choose.'"

Kirkpatrick continued her intellectual pursuits, doing freelance work as a research associate for a political science professor at Amherst College. Again, she did research on communism, for a venture called the "Communism in government" project, supported by the Fund for the Republic, a private organization.

Kirkpatrick's husband—as well as most other Americans—shared her concern with Communist aggression. By 1955, Communist governments were ruling not only the Soviet Union but also East Germany, Czechoslovakia, Poland, Romania, Hungary, Bul-

garia, China, and North Korea. In 1956, Evron Kirkpatrick edited a book on Communist movements called *Target: The World*. In it, he warned, "Wherever Communism has come to power it has demanded total control over the actions and minds of all whom it rules." In an effort to explain why so many people were attracted to communism, he chose to examine the movement's use of propaganda.

When her son Douglas was almost two, Kirkpatrick gave birth to another son, John; and a year and a half later, she had Stuart. By then, the Kirkpatricks had moved to Bethesda, Maryland. There they bought a house for their growing family. With a new, larger home and three young children, Kirkpatrick was extremely busy. Later, she referred to this period of her life as her "years of intensive childbearing." At the same time, she put her motto Refuse to Choose into action and did not neglect her career. She applied her intellectual skills in her freelance job and decided that her economic goal was to make enough money to pay for household help. She preferred to spend her time at home caring for her children instead of cleaning the house.

Kirkpatrick later implied that her years of mothering may have aided her scholarship. She told a reporter from *Newsweek*: "Truth, which is important to a scholar, has got to be concrete. And there is nothing more concrete than dealing with babies, with burps and bottles, frogs and mud."

When she was not doing freelance work or taking care of her children,

The three Kirkpatrick boys, (left to right) John, Stuart, and Douglas,
visited Split Rock, Pennsylvania, in 1968 with their grandparents
Leona and Welcher Jordan. The Jordans enjoyed spending time with
their grandchildren.

Kirkpatrick found time to be involved with national politics. In 1960, the Kirkpatricks' friend Hubert Humphrey made a brief campaign for the Democratic nomination for the presidency but withdrew when it became clear that John F. Kennedy would get the nomination. Kirkpatrick and her husband supported Kennedy and his running mate Lyndon B. Johnson against the Republican candidate, Richard M. Nixon. They traveled to Los Angeles, California, to attend the Democratic National Convention there, which was essentially a party-wide show of unity for Kennedy.

In the fall of 1962, when her youngest son had started nursery school, Kirkpatrick began working outside her home again, at Trinity College, a small women's college in Washington. A Catholic college operated by the Sisters of Notre Dame de Namur, Trinity is located on a pleasant, wooded 34-acre campus about 26 miles from downtown Washington. Kirkpatrick was appointed to a half-time position as an assistant professor of political science. Her hours, however, were longer than those of many full-time professors: She taught for two hours four mornings a week.

While she was teaching at Trinity, Kirkpatrick published her first book, *The Strategy of Deception: A Study in World-wide Communist Tactics.* Continuing her longtime interest in nondemocratic governments, she assembled essays by prominent scholars on how Communist parties outside the Soviet Union had achieved power in such diverse countries as China, Czechoslovakia, and Cuba. In the book's introduction, she stated her firm belief: "The means by which Communist parties have come to power do not suggest either democracy or progress."

There was ample reason at the time to be worried about the spread of communism. Nikita Khrushchev, the leader of the Soviet Union, was aggressively predicting that Communist regimes would eventually rule the world. Many felt that the Communist, totalitarian Soviet Union had nothing in common with the capitalist, demo-

A view from the choir shows the chapel at Trinity College in Washington, D.C. In 1962, Kirkpatrick won an appointment as an assistant professor of political science and taught eight hours a week but still found time to complete her first published book, The Strategy of Deception, *while she was there.*

cratic United States and, in fact, would vigorously oppose U.S. policy and U.S. allies everywhere in an hostile effort to expand its influence. Wherever the interests of the two nations, known as the superpowers, collided, the threat of war appeared to loom. When Fidel Castro came to power in the Cuban revolution of 1959, identified himself as a Communist, and formed an alliance between Cuba—only 90 miles from the United States—and the Soviet Union, Americans were frightened at the prospect of war between the Soviet Union and the United States. In 1961, Americans were even more worried about the conflict between the Soviet Union and the United States over Germany.

After Germany's defeat in World War II, the Allies had partitioned Germany into four zones, with the western section controlled by the British, Americans, and French, and the eastern section controlled by the Soviets. Berlin, a city more than 100 miles within the East German border, was controlled by all four countries. During the postwar period, Western Europe had become more allied with the United States, partly as a result of the Marshall Plan. While the West was coalescing into a bloc of more or less allied nations, the Soviets were becoming more fearful of a strengthened Germany, to whom they had suffered enormous losses during World War II. They sought to control part of Germany and separate it from Western Europe. In 1949, the Soviet Union announced the creation of the German Democratic Republic (often called East Germany)

out of the part of Germany they supervised; they solidified Communist control over half of Berlin, formalizing the existence of two Germanys and two Berlins. The United States refused to recognize the new country, and the two superpowers continued to struggle over the divided Germany and divided Berlin. Meanwhile, nearly 3 million people from the east streamed into the western zone between 1945 and 1961.

In 1961, as people from East Berlin poured at an ever-increasing rate from that Communist city into non-Communist West Berlin, Khrushchev ordered construction of a wall—28 miles of barbed wire and concrete blocks—to seal the border between the two cities. In the years that followed, the Berlin Wall became one of the most poignant symbols of the conflict between the Soviet Union and the United States, which came to be known as the cold war.

When President Kennedy visited West Berlin in 1963, he made a powerful speech about the wall: "There are many people in the world who really don't understand, or say they don't, what is the great issue between the free world and the Communist world. Let them come to Berlin. There are some who say that communism is the wave of the future. Let them come to Berlin. And there are even a few who say that it is true that communism is an evil system, but it permits us to make economic progress. . . . Let them come to Berlin. Freedom has many difficulties and democracy is not perfect, but we have never had to put up a wall to keep our people in, to prevent them from leaving us."

During this period, as tensions rose between the United States and the Soviet Union, many Americans feared nuclear war would break out between the two countries, and some Americans built fallout shelters where they could protect themselves from the deadly effects of radiation from a nuclear blast. In late October 1962, it seemed those fallout shelters might be needed.

At 7:00 P.M., October 22, President Kennedy went on national television and announced that the United States learned that the Soviets had, for the first time, placed offensive weapons outside their country, in Cuba. Kennedy announced a U.S. naval blockade of any further shipments of offensive arms from the Soviet Union to Cuba and increased U.S. surveillance of the island. The most ominous part of his statement ran, "It shall be the policy of this nation to regard any nuclear missile launched from Cuba against any nation in the Western Hemisphere as an attack by the Soviet Union on the United States, requiring a full retaliatory response upon the Soviet Union." The nation stood on the brink of war.

Kennedy ordered the U.S. Army's airborne divisions to prepare for deployment, and 100,000 U.S. Army troops gathered in Florida. At the UN, U.S. Ambassador Adlai Stevenson said to the Security Council: "Since the end of the Second World War, there has been no threat to the vision of peace so profound. . . . The hopes of mankind are concentrated in this room."

Like most Americans, Kirkpatrick watched the events of the Cuban missile crisis with mounting fear and horror. She wondered whether she and her husband should have built a fallout shelter in their backyard. Finally, after several tense days, Premier Khrushchev agreed to dismantle and remove the missiles from Cuba. "It was the most dangerous time," Kirkpatrick said later, "the closest to war that we've come in the post–World War II period."

Less than a year later, the nation was jolted again when President Kennedy—popular, young, and admired—was assassinated in Dallas, Texas, on November 22, 1963. Like so many of her generation, Kirkpatrick remembered exactly where she was when she heard the news that stunned the nation: at the hairdresser's, in a shopping center near her home. A few hours later, Vice-president Lyndon Johnson was sworn in as president on Air Force One, the official presidential plane that carried Kennedy's body back to Washington.

When Johnson ran for reelection in 1964, he chose Hubert Humphrey as his running mate. The Kirkpatricks again attended the Democratic National Convention, held that year in Atlantic City, New Jersey, where they worked together on Humphrey's speeches. During the campaign, they analyzed polls for Humphrey, a skill Kirkpatrick had acquired in her job at George Washington University. In November, Johnson and Humphrey went on to a landslide victory, winning 61 percent of the vote.

President John Kennedy inspects a battery of missiles in Key West, Florida, during the Cuban missile crisis, when the Soviet Union installed nuclear missiles in Cuba. Kirkpatrick commented on the period, "It was the most dangerous time, the closest to war that we've come in the post–World War II period."

Kirkpatrick soon decided to return to full-time work outside her home, a job that would prove as rewarding as that early position at George Washington. In 1967, when her youngest son was eight, after five years of part-time teaching at Trinity, she won an appointment to a full-time post at Georgetown University. She would be an associate professor of political science there. Although very few women professors taught at Georgetown, the political science department did have one other woman on its faculty, and she had achieved tenure. In just a few years, Kirkpatrick became only the second woman to earn tenure at what she later called "the best university in the Washington area, with the best political science department in the Washington area." It was quite an achievement, but it was certainly not to be her last.

Kirkpatrick pauses to muse in her office at Georgetown in 1980. During the previous two decades Kirkpatrick earned her doctorate from Columbia University, became a tenured professor at Georgetown University, and wrote several books. Despite her immersion in the academic world, she never ignored the startling developments in U.S. politics throughout the era.

SIX

Political Woman

Georgetown University, where Kirkpatrick found her intellectual home, was established in 1789, the same year that the U.S. Constitution was written and that George Washington was inaugurated as the country's first president. In keeping with its beginning, the university's history is rich with patriotism. Georgetown's school colors, for example, are blue and gray, the colors that signified the North and South, respectively, during the Civil War. Following the war, Georgetown adopted these colors to symbolize the union of North and South into one nation.

A Roman Catholic university directed by the Jesuit order, Georgetown is the oldest Catholic school of higher learning in the United States. Located on a hilltop overlooking the Potomac River in the Georgetown section of Washington, it is surrounded by attractive town houses, seemingly removed from the modern bustle of downtown Washington and its imposing government offices. Many Georgetown graduates eventually find their way into the corridors and halls of government, particularly the Department of State. After World War I, Georgetown established a school of foreign service, highly esteemed as one of the finest training grounds in the nation for career diplomats. Although Kirkpatrick did not teach in the foreign service school, many of its students took her courses.

In this internationally oriented atmosphere, Kirkpatrick's work as a professor and writer flourished. Despite her commitment to teaching—she insisted on doing her own work, without the researchers or assistants that other professors employed, and graded all examinations by herself—she found time to pursue her own intellectual interests as well as to maintain an active role in the sphere of national politics.

Years after she began researching her doctoral dissertation, she had started to write it at Trinity. At age 41, she completed her writing and received a doctorate in political science from Columbia in 1968. She abandoned her earlier topic—communism in France—and chose to investigate another non-democratic political movement. She decided to explore the rise to power of Juan Domingo Perón, a former military leader who was elected president of Argentina in 1946 and who intermittently dominated Argentine politics until his death in 1975. Kirkpatrick's study was later published as a book, *Leader and Vanguard in Mass Society: A Study of Peronist Argentina*, by the MIT (Massachusetts Institute of Technology) Press.

"For the student of nondemocratic regimes Latin America is an especially fruitful scene for research," she wrote in her introduction. She was interested in how Perón and his wife Evita had organized the lower classes of Argentina to support them in the movement that came to be known as "Peronism." From 1946 to 1955, the Peróns managed Argentina's economy to provide higher salaries and better benefits for workers, but they also destroyed the independence of labor unions and suppressed dissent.

An open admirer of the Italian Fascist Mussolini, Perón had a strong dislike for the United States and espoused what he referred to as the Third Position—an economic system between communism and capitalism. Kirkpatrick believed that Peronism was especially important because movements like it might be replicated in other Latin American countries.

In Peronism, Kirkpatrick also found a subject that allowed her to investigate another interest: the political behavior of common people. Although political scientists often wrote about the experience of presidents and kings, they frequently ignored the lives of the lower classes. She wanted her study to accurately reflect the experience of Peronists—who were ordinary people—so she put the social science skills she had learned at George Washington to work by using a series of questionnaires in which she asked Argentinians about their lives under the leadership of Juan Perón.

Kirkpatrick discovered that Perón's supporters were much more concerned with concrete economic issues than with other political questions and that they wanted a strong leader. Peronists were not much interested in foreign policy issues—which they said they did not understand—and they tended to blame the government for not informing them about foreign policy.

When she was finishing her dissertation on Peronism, Kirkpatrick traveled to New York City several times to meet with her advisers at Columbia. The school, like the rest of the country, was in turmoil in 1967 and 1968.

Johnson was in the White House, and Humphrey was vice-president. Their administration was widely criticized

Kirkpatrick gave the commencement address at Georgetown in 1981. When she joined the faculty there in 1968, she was one of only two female professors in the political science department.

by Americans who opposed U.S. military involvement in North and South Vietnam, two countries created in 1954 from former French colonies that shared the eastern edge of the Indochinese peninsula. North and South Vietnam's history was even more tumultuous and complex than North and South Korea's, but like those two countries, the North had a Communist government and the South had an elected regime backed by the United States.

In the early 1960s, the North Vietnamese began to aggressively support Communist guerrillas and insurgents in the South who sought to overthrow the government there. The North spearheaded the formation of a Communist-led coalition, called the National Liberation Front (NLF), which did have some support in the South. In response, the United States stepped up its aid and sent military advisers to South Vietnam, in keeping with its policies of protecting non-Communist

67

governments from overthrow by Communists.

Johnson had ordered aerial bombing of North Vietnamese targets in February 1965 and then escalated the war in Vietnam dramatically, sending more and more U.S. troops to fight the Communist regime of North Vietnam. Because the NLF's military forces (known as the Vietcong in the South) controlled many rural areas in the South, much of South Vietnam was also devastated in an attempt to root out the Vietcong. By February 1968, nearly 1.5 million South Vietnamese were homeless refugees. Fighting also affected the impoverished nations surrounding the two Vietnams, including Cambodia, Laos, and Thailand. In the end, the United States's involvement changed more than the Indochinese peninsula's tragic history; it also profoundly affected U.S. society and politics.

American sentiment against the war increased as Johnson stepped up the bombing of North Vietnam. The financial cost to the United States was high—almost $30 billion a year by 1968—but the toll in lives was also high and harder to bear, for between 1961 and 1967, almost 16,000 U.S. military personnel were killed; 100,000 were wounded. Between January and June of 1968, nearly 40,000 college students at more than 100 U.S. campuses protested against continued involvement in the war. Finally, on March 31, 1968, Johnson appeared on national television and announced a halt to most of the bombing. He also said he would not run for reelection that No-

vember. The war went on, however, and antiwar activists continued calling for unconditional withdrawal of all U.S. troops. The difference of opinion regarding the war had become particularly bitter by the spring of 1968.

A few days after Johnson's historic double-barreled announcement, the nation was shocked again. On April 4, Martin Luther King, Jr.—the black civil rights leader and 1964 winner of the Nobel Peace Prize who organized nonviolent protests against racial segregation—was assassinated in Memphis, Tennessee. Following his murder, rioting broke out in Baltimore, Chicago, Hartford, Newark, and Pittsburgh. The death toll reached 39, and almost 20,000 people were arrested. Federal troops patrolled the streets of Washington, D.C., enforcing a strict curfew.

Less than a month later, on April 23, radical students at Columbia University occupied several administration buildings and effectively closed down the university for six and a half days. During the strike, Kirkpatrick had to deliver her dissertation to Columbia's Low Library. Because of the unrest and disorder, she had to make her way there through the underground tunnels beneath the university. Later, she talked about the student radicals. "In the name of democracy, they were engaged in a violent attack on free speech. One of my friends on the faculty, for example, narrowly missed being hit on the head by the brass nozzle of a fire hose and had to escape into the basement of a building. Another faculty member I knew had his office destroyed. This was bad stuff, fascist behavior."

During the strike at Columbia—in an unrelated event—Humphrey announced his candidacy for president. Senators Eugene McCarthy and Robert F. Kennedy had already entered the race for the Democratic nomination and were attracting young people and liberals who were against the war. Humphrey drew people such as the Kirkpatricks, who were longtime Democrats—the party faithful.

The race for the Democratic nomination soon narrowed tragically. In June, Kennedy was assassinated in California, after winning the primary there. President Johnson ordered Secret Service protection for all presidential candidates for the first time in American history. Americans were stunned by the assassination of two prominent men within three months of each other. Turbulent antiwar demonstrations continued, riots ripped apart the cities, and the nation looked on in horror.

By the time the Democratic National Convention was held in late August, the country had been besieged by shocking news for months, but no relief was forthcoming. The Democratic convention in Chicago was the scene of some of the year's most violent demonstrations. Inside the convention, Humphrey was branded a warmonger when he refused to support the party's peace platform. McCarthy supporters and other antiwar activists wanted unconditional, unilateral U.S. withdrawal

Juan Perón was president of Argentina from 1946 to 1955 and returned briefly to power there in 1973 until his death in 1974. Kirkpatrick wrote her doctoral dissertation about his and his supporters' influence on Argentine politics.

from Vietnam; Humphrey favored a negotiated settlement in which U.S. action depended on reciprocal action by the North Vietnamese. The party failed to adopt the peace platform, and antiwar Democrats grew angrier. Outside the convention, bloody confrontations between militant students and the Chicago police continued. Television cameras carried the scene around the globe as the students chanted, "The whole world is watching, the whole world is watching." The eyes of the world did not deter the Chicago police from giving particularly brutal beatings to and using tear gas on unarmed protesters; nor did they deter violent protesters from harassing innocent delegates and others at the convention.

Kirkpatrick, her husband, and their oldest son attended the convention, staying at the Palmer House and work-

Kirkpatrick's efforts to deliver her dissertation to Columbia University met with unexpected delays in 1968. On April 30, student demonstrators formed a human barricade around Columbia and called for a student-faculty strike and the resignation of the university administration. Their actions were a response to a predawn police raid, condoned by the school, that resulted in the arrest of hundreds of student activists who had occupied university buildings since April 23.

ing during the day at the Conrad Hilton, analyzing polls for Humphrey. Kirkpatrick described the experience later. "One of the Weatherpeople [the Weathermen were a militant antiwar group] put uric acid in the air conditioning system in the Palmer House and the Hilton Hotel, so one lived for days with the smell of stale vomit." Like many people, she was shocked at the violence in Chicago. "It was a searing experience, very traumatic," she said later. "It was a real assault on democratic freedom."

The Democratic party in 1968 was still controlled by the party regulars, who supported Humphrey, and he won the nomination. But the party was deeply divided, not only over the war but also over delegate selection and control of the party. McCarthy supporters felt the party was closed to newcomers, and before the convention ended, the party had resolved to open up the 1972 convention to more recent participants in party politics.

The Kirkpatricks campaigned for Humphrey, but he lost the election by a tiny margin to Richard M. Nixon, whose campaign was the most expensive in the country's history. Kirkpatrick reflected later on Humphrey's loss. "I expected that Humphrey would lose. It was too bad. He would have made a very good president."

She did not blame the antiwar activists for Humphrey's loss, however, but Lyndon Johnson. Before he decided not to run again, Johnson had set the convention date in late August, to coincide with his birthday, hoping perhaps for a birthday tribute. "That's very late for a convention," Kirkpatrick said later. "It leaves very little time between the nomination and the election. At that point, the Democratic National Committee was broke. Johnson had not raised money for the campaign. If he had remained the candidate, it wouldn't have been so bad, because if you're an incumbent president, the money rolls in. As vice-president, Humphrey couldn't begin a campaign until the convention. What was needed more than anything else was time and money."

Kirkpatrick's disillusionment with the Democratic party had begun, but she was willing to stay in the party and try to change it. In the meantime, she and her family left the United States to spend the year of 1969 in the south of France.

Evron Kirkpatrick had become president of the board of trustees of the Institute of American Universities, an organization based in Aix-en-Provence, in France. The institute arranged for American students to study in France while they continued their non-French academic work. In connection with this work, Kirkpatrick and her husband visited Aix and decided they would like to spend a year there. She arranged to take a sabbatical from Georgetown, and the family departed. (Professors are often granted sabbaticals—extended time off from teaching—so that they can pursue their own research in depth.) The Kirkpatricks rented a house near Mount St. Victoire, which had been a favorite subject of the great 19th-century painter Paul Cézanne, and immersed themselves in French life.

In Washington, Kirkpatrick's sons attended the Sidwell Friends School, a prestigious private school run by the American Friends Service Committee. (Members of the Society of Friends are often called Quakers. Among their beliefs is pacificism.) "We kept ourselves financially on the brink for many years paying tuition," Kirkpatrick said later. Neither parent minded the sacrifice, for as intellectuals they highly valued education. In Aix, the Kirkpatricks promptly enrolled their sons at a French boys' school and arranged for a tutor to help them learn the new language and find their way around the school. The playground of a French school, it turned out, was much different from that of an American Friends school; the Kirkpatrick boys began to suffer at the hands of their classmates. "They were coming home with bloody noses and torn shirts," Kirkpatrick said later. "I wanted to take them out of the school. My husband pointed out that they hadn't asked to be taken out. He said we ought to wait and give them a chance to succeed. That was one of the times I recognized how important it was for boys to have a father's perspective." After a time, the boys did succeed and took pleasure in the accomplishment of a difficult task— adapting to a foreign environment. When the Kirkpatricks returned to Aix for a second sabbatical year in 1974, the boys adjusted easily.

After their sojourn in France, Kirkpatrick and her family returned to Washington and plunged back into politics. In 1972, Humphrey again vied for the Democratic presidential nomination, but this time, he lost—to George McGovern, who attracted the liberal, antiwar faction of the party.

Following McGovern's nomination, Kirkpatrick and her husband helped organize the CDM to counter the McGovern supporters, seen by many as party liberals. Many members of the CDM were former Humphrey supporters or backers of Senator Henry "Scoop" Jackson. Some members represented labor unions, and many were intellectuals. After the Democratic convention, they began to meet at a club in downtown Washington, but stayed quiet until after the election. "Nobody wanted to sound a note of opposition to the Democratic nominee in the course of the campaign," Kirkpatrick said. "That would have been very bad politics. But we got ready to announce after the election. We were all absolutely certain that McGovern was going to be very badly beaten."

McGovern was badly beaten, garnering electoral votes from only Massachusetts and the District of Columbia. It was the worst defeat in American history for a Democratic presidential candidate. Kirkpatrick herself voted Republican for the first time in her life. Later, in the first article she wrote for *Commentary*, she analyzed why Nixon had won by such a landslide. "Senator McGovern's basic problem in the Presidential campaign was an inability to establish identification with traditional American cultural values," she

Hubert H. Humphrey greets supporters in Nashville, Tennessee, during his 1968 campaign for president. Despite a turbulent convention and campaign, he attracted widespread support but lost the election by a very small margin.

wrote. She argued that McGovern represented the values of the counterculture—the culture that coalesced around student activism, riots in the cities, and the antiwar movement. Kirkpatrick thought a different candidate might have been able to divorce the Vietnam war from cultural issues and been "better able to turn popular discontent over the war to electoral advantage." But McGovern symbolized more than antiwar sentiment, she argued; he represented new cultural values that most Americans found repugnant.

The 1972 presidential election was historic not only because of Nixon's landslide victory but also for the values held by the incumbent president, which the country soon learned about when the *Washington Post* broke the Watergate scandal. In 1968, Nixon had narrowly defeated Humphrey; he was determined to win big in 1972. With

Left to right: *Douglas, John, Evron, Jeane, and Stuart Kirkpatrick at dinner outdoors in the south of France. In 1968 and 1974, the Kirkpatricks lived in Aix-en-Provence while Evron supervised the Institute of American Universities there. The years in France gave the family exciting opportunities to travel and study in Europe.*

Nixon's reelection as their goal and on his behalf, five men burglarized the headquarters of the Democratic National Committee in the Watergate Hotel. Although the burglars were arrested, the White House successfully and illegally impeded investigation of their crimes until after Nixon was reelected. When the White House cover-up became public, the Nixon administration unraveled, and he was forced to resign in August 1974.

Reflecting on the Watergate years, Kirkpatrick said, "I found the behavior of the Nixon White House incredibly stupid. It was the work of people who didn't understand politics. Anybody who understood politics would have known there wasn't anything that was valuable in the basement of the Democratic National Committee." She was outraged that a president would break the law, abusing both his office and the trust of the American people.

At the time of the Watergate scandal, Kirkpatrick was spending much of her time investigating the subject of women in government. She asked, Why aren't more women participating in the highest level of politics? Answering that question led her to write *Political Woman*, the first major study of women in American politics. With its publication, her work gained an audience outside the academic community for the first time.

"Political man is a familiar figure with a long history," she wrote in the first chapter. "As chief, prince, king, counsellor, premier, president, dictator, chairman he has led, battled, pillaged, conquered, built, judged, governed. Political man has fascinated and challenged historians and philosophers; he has been described, dissected, praised, excoriated and psychoanalyzed."

She noted the absence of women at the upper echelons of American politics, pointing out that 50 years after ratification of the 19th Amendment to the Constitution, which occurred in 1920 and allowed women to vote, "no woman has been nominated to be president or vice-president, no woman has served on the Supreme Court. Today, there is no woman in the cabinet, no woman in the Senate, no woman serving as governor of a major state, no woman mayor of a major city, no woman in the top leadership of either major party."

With his daughter Julie and her husband David Eisenhower (on the right) and his daughter Tricia and her husband Edward Cox (on the left), Nixon bids his cabinet and White House staff farewell at his resignation on August 9, 1974. Rather than face impeachment for impeding the investigation of the burglary of Democratic headquarters, Nixon resigned; he was later granted a full pardon by his successor, Gerald Ford.

The situation for women in politics was beginning to change, she noted. The women's movement was pressing for expanded roles for women, pointing out that women need not be nurses instead of doctors or schoolteachers instead of college professors, and the social penalties—which ranged from disapproval to outright hostility—for not conforming to traditional roles were decreasing. But at the highest levels of government, women were still absent.

To find women in politics, Kirkpatrick looked at state legislatures and chose 46 women to study. Although men dominated that level of government, too, women had served as legislators since 1921. By 1972, there were 457 women in the national total of 7,700 state legislators. Who are these women? Kirkpatrick asked. What, if anything, do they have in common? Did they pay a personal price for victory? Why are there so few women in politics?

She found that political women were not much different from other women. They married, had children, and carried out the traditional roles of wife and mother. Unlike other women, though, their definitions of "femininity" were broad enough to include the role of politician. The 46 legislators believed they could be good wives and mothers and also hold public office, whereas other women and men tended to think such role combinations were almost impossible. The behavior of women legislators also resembled that of their male counterparts, with one important exception. They often chose to begin their political careers later, after their children had started school. Kirkpatrick concluded that the main reason more women did not enter politics was prevailing role definitions.

Considering the future of women in politics, she was cautiously optimistic. "The obstacles to the achievement of de facto political equality of the sexes are enormous," she wrote. "They make its achievement in the near future very unlikely. Far more likely is the continuation of existing trends toward gradual inclusion of women in power processes." In light of her future appointment as ambassador, it is interesting that she called for government to aid and speed the development of women's participation in politics by appointing more women to high positions.

Political Woman was hailed as "exceptionally lucid and intelligent" by one critic. Another said it was "perceptive, realistic, wise, well read, and often witty." With this book, Kirkpatrick began to be recognized as an expert on women in politics. In 1975, she was asked by the U.S. Information Agency to represent the United States at a conference held in west Africa to celebrate International Women's Year. There she spoke on women's participation in public affairs and also traveled to four other countries, where she lectured on the American political system.

Kirkpatrick went on to write another book about women in politics, but this time she focused on the national level.

Like *Political Woman*, her next book—*The New Presidential Elite: Men and Women in National Politics*—was well received, but coverage of its publication was more limited to academic journals.

In *The New Presidential Elite*, Kirkpatrick described the delegates to the 1972 Democratic and Republican conventions, when the Democrats nominated McGovern and the Republicans nominated Nixon. She believed that the political events of 1972 were part of a continuing transformation in American politics: that occurrences such as the Democrats' sweeping reformation of their party rules and the appearance of direct action—sit-ins and demonstrations—"argue that the American political system is undergoing quite fundamental changes." The reforms in the Democratic party, Kirkpatrick thought, were weakening it; the Democratic delegates did not represent the voters. She wrote that "1972 Democratic delegates were less representative of the views and values of voters than were delegates to the 'unreformed' Republican Convention, and the 'new' political type concentrated in the McGovern ranks were least representative of all."

On the other hand, she noted that there were more women delegates at the 1972 Democratic convention than there had been in 1968—up from 13 percent to 39 percent—and that there were more blacks at the convention. However, even though the Democrats appeared to have filled their quotas for women, blacks, and youth, "it remained true," Kirkpatrick wrote, "that a majority of both conventions were male, white, and middle-aged."

The book aided Kirkpatrick's thriving career. Soon after *The New Presidential Elite* came out, William Baroody, Sr., the president of the American Enterprise Institute (AEI) approached her about joining their staff. The AEI is one of the country's oldest "think tanks"—an institute in which scholars are paid to think and write about public policies—and Kirkpatrick had several friends there, including Antonin Scalia, who was later appointed to the U.S. Supreme Court. The AEI was rich with intellectuals from diverse backgrounds, giving it an atmosphere similar to that of her earlier job at George Washington University. "There were people in theology and economics and constitutional law and intellectual history," Kirkpatrick noted with pleasure.

She accepted Baroody's offer to spend a sabbatical year, 1977, at the AEI. After that year, she remained on the staff, doing the writing and research that she had previously done at home in her office at the AEI. "I was very interested in the whole intellectual milieu of AEI," she said later. "I found it stimulating. And they offer research support, including library facilities at your fingertips and secretarial help, which is harder to come by in a university."

Kirkpatrick was the first woman to serve as a senior scholar at the AEI. She would remain there for many years, as the institute flourished and published her work. The AEI's revenue had grown to more than $10 million by 1988, most of which came from contributions from corporations and foundations. This money supported not only its operating expenses but also an extensive publishing program. By 1989, the AEI had published more than 2,000 books, including works on public health, foreign policy, economics, and international trade.

Kirkpatrick had become a well-known writer and scholar. She had tenure at Georgetown and a prestigious post at a Washington research center. Then, in 1978 and 1979, her life began to change, both for personal and professional reasons.

She had remained close to her parents and brother through the years, visiting and speaking with them often. Her brother, a prominent attorney in Columbus, Ohio, was married and had three children. Jerry Jordan had grieved along with Kirkpatrick when their father, who was almost 75 years old, died in 1974. Four years later, they began to worry about their mother.

Kirkpatrick traveled back to Stephens College in May 1978 to receive its Distinguished Alumna Award and give the commencement address. The commencement was held on Mother's Day, and her mother attended the ceremony, delighted at this latest

McGovern accepts the Democratic nomination for president on August 14, 1972, in Miami, Florida. Kirkpatrick's 1976 book, The New Presidential Elite, *about the delegates who attended that convention, so impressed the director of the American Enterprise Institute, William Baroody, that he invited her to join the staff.*

of her daughter's achievements. Kirkpatrick watched her mother and thought she seemed more tired than usual, because she had to sit down and rest frequently. Kirkpatrick returned home to Washington but became even more concerned when her mother said she was ill with the flu. Wasting no time, Kirkpatrick flew to Illinois and found her mother very weak. She took her to St. Louis for tests, stayed with her at the hospital, and then took her back to Mount Vernon. When Kirkpatrick returned to Washington, her mother's doctor called with the news: Mrs. Jordan had leukemia, the kind that was invariably fatal.

"That was an awful telephone conversation," Kirkpatrick said later. "From that point, I understood that my mother was going to die before too long." Although her mother was aged—as an old-fashioned southern lady, she tended to refer vaguely to herself as "in her eighties"—the news came as a shock. She had always been extremely important to Kirkpatrick. Now they would have one winter together before she died. Mrs. Jordan spent much of the winter in Washington, at Kirkpatrick's home. "But she was always eager to go home to her house," Kirkpatrick said. Her mother died in April 1979.

Soon thereafter, Kirkpatrick published her widely read article "Dictatorships and Double Standards" in *Commentary* magazine. Jimmy Carter had been president for three years, and she thought his foreign policies were misguided. Pro-American autocracies, she argued, such as the one headed by Anastasio Somoza in Nicaragua, deserved U.S. support more than did totalitarian governments that were anti-U.S. With continued U.S. support, Somoza's government, she suggested, might have gradually instituted democratic reforms, such as free elections and an uncensored press. By contrast, totalitarian governments, such as the one set up by the Sandinistas, who overthrew Somoza, were not likely to evolve toward democracy, she said. There was no instance in history up to that point of a Communist government becoming more democratic. These were the ideas often called the Kirkpatrick Doctrine.

Kirkpatrick's article made her objections to Carter's foreign policy loud and clear, and she published it with trepidation. "I thought the sky was going to fall on me," she told a writer from *Vogue* magazine.

The sky did not fall, of course, but Kirkpatrick's life did change dramatically in the months after her article was published. Presidential candidate Ronald Reagan read it and drafted her to join his campaign. Several months later, he asked her to become ambassador to the UN. Soon she took a leave from Georgetown and the AEI and moved to New York. The scholar and professor, the political woman, became an international leader, one whose views and actions affected world events.

Kirkpatrick acted forcefully at the UN in an effort to strengthen the U.S. position in the organization. She felt that smaller countries were taking advantage of the United States by engaging in unwarranted criticism of U.S. policies and allies. Several times, she spoke favorably of withdrawing financial support from UN agencies that opposed the goals of the United States.

SEVEN

Permanent Ambassador to the United Nations

Kirkpatrick assumed her duties as permanent U.S. ambassador to the UN in January 1981, becoming the first woman in U.S. history to hold the post. Packing only a few belongings—among them her beloved recordings of Bach—she moved into the ambassador's official residence at the Waldorf Towers in Manhattan and began shuttling back and forth between Washington and New York. In Washington, she consulted with the president, attended meetings of his cabinet, or top advisers, and met with the National Security Planning Group, which advises the president on foreign policy issues.

In New York, where she spent four days a week, Kirkpatrick rose at 6:30 A.M., showered, and read cables and newspapers while breakfasting on half a grapefruit and a cup of tea. While her

hair dried, she made phone calls until almost 9:00 A.M. A little before nine, she left for the UN, not returning home until after the obligatory dinner party and often not going to bed until 1:00 A.M., after an hour of reading.

At the UN, Kirkpatrick oversaw a staff of about 130 people. For her senior staff, she chose people with strong academic backgrounds, most of them Ph.D.s, who were experts in specific fields. José Sorzano, for example, was a refugee from Castro's Cuba and a graduate of Georgetown's political philosophy program. "He had a bilingual, bicultural background," Kirkpatrick said later. She wanted people on her staff who understood other cultures and spoke languages other than English. Kirkpatrick herself spoke French and Spanish, having learned Spanish on her own. Another staff member was born in Austria, and German was his first language. She also hired a media expert, Charles Lichenstein, who had been vice-president of the Corporation for Public Broadcasting, the public television network. Some of her staff members were Democrats, and others were Republicans, but Kirkpatrick was not greatly concerned with party affiliation. An aide to the president told her, however, that she could not "fill the place with Democrats."

Several months after she became ambassador, Kirkpatrick faced her first test. On June 7, Israel bombed a nuclear reactor in Iraq, maintaining that the attack was necessary to prevent Iraq from manufacturing nuclear weapons to be used against Israel. As international peacekeeper, the UN had to condemn the attack. Israel, however, was one of the United States's closest allies, and Kirkpatrick was a strong defender of Israel. Using superb negotiating skills, she achieved a compromise resolution that condemned the attack but imposed no penalties, or sanctions, on Israel. The resolution was widely viewed as a triumph of diplomacy and earned praise from President Reagan, who called Kirkpatrick a "heroine." Iraq's foreign minister, Saadoon Hammadi, the respected diplomat with whom Kirkpatrick negotiated the compromise, also praised her. In a *Newsweek* article, Hammadi was quoted as saying, "One Kirkpatrick was equal to more than two men. Maybe three."

Kirkpatrick said later that she had regrets about having to condemn Israel.

In a widely published photograph, her hand was barely raised as she voted for the resolution she had negotiated. Some of her old friends at *Commentary*, which is published by the American Jewish Committee, were apparently angry at her about the resolution. Even within the Reagan administration, Kirkpatrick's actions drew criticism.

Alexander M. Haig, Jr., who had served with the Nixon administration, was then secretary of state. Two of his aides told reporters that Kirkpatrick had mishandled the Israel-Iraq matter and that Haig had come to the rescue, saving Israel from UN sanctions. The *New York Times* then featured a headline reading, MRS. KIRKPATRICK FAULTED ON IRAQ BY HAIG'S AIDES.

Although Haig subsequently retracted the statements made by his deputies, saying they were misinformed, many observers attributed the skirmish to Haig's jealousy of Kirkpatrick. As head of the Department of State, he was her boss at the UN, but in meetings of the cabinet and of the National Security Planning Group meetings, they were equals. In addition, whereas her popularity with the American people was growing, his was declining.

After the Israel-Iraq crisis, Kirkpatrick dealt firmly with another problem: U.S. bashing by the small nations of the UN. In its early years, the UN was dominated by the larger countries that helped form it: the United States, the Soviet Union, Britain, China, and France. But by 1981 the organization

Kirkpatrick is sworn in as U.S. ambassador to the UN on February 4, 1981. She was the first woman to hold that post.

had changed considerably. Total membership had more than tripled, from 51 nations in 1950 to 158 in 1983. During the 1960s and 1970s, the growth included many of the small nations in Asia, Africa, and the Caribbean that were formerly colonies of European countries. These small, less developed countries are known as Third World nations. They responded to the rivalry between the United States and the Soviet Union and the conflicting pressures the superpowers placed on them by banding together to form a group called the nonaligned nations. By 1981 the nonaligned nations had become highly critical of U.S. policies, even though many of them received aid from the United States. *New York* magazine quoted Kirkpatrick about the reason why: "If you are a small country in the U.N. and you know there's going to be a price for opposing the Soviet bloc or the Cuban-dominated non-aligned bloc, and no price for opposing the U.S., you will oppose the U.S., obviously."

Before Kirkpatrick became ambassador, the United States had often ignored criticism from the Third World, or non-aligned countries. Several European diplomats and some members of the Department of State felt that it was permissible for Third World nations to "blow off steam" by indulging in harsh, violent rhetoric in the UN. After all, the reasoning went, these small nations had little real power. Kirkpatrick spoke about the turnabout in the U.S. attitude during a 1989 interview: "In the early days of the U.N., the Americans were

Kirkpatrick chats with Ambassador Yu of China (far right) in Geneva at a meeting of the Economic and Social Council (ECOSOC) of the UN in 1981. While at the UN most of her time was taken up with travel and numerous work-related social activities.

the ones who took it seriously. Eleanor Roosevelt, for example, led discussions in the Human Rights Commission that were enormously important." But in recent years the United States had abandoned the UN, Kirkpatrick thought, to the leaders of the non-aligned movement. In an interview with Linda Fasulo, who put together a book, *Representing America*, about the experiences of 33 American diplomats and representatives at the UN, Kirkpatrick said, "I believe that U.S. influence at the United Nations has been frittered away." She had no intention of allowing the process to go any further.

In late September of 1981, a group of ambassadors from the nonaligned nations issued a communiqué that attacked various U.S. policies. They said the United States was preventing disarmament, supporting Zionism (the movement for advancing the state of Israel), and continuing its colonial rule of Puerto Rico. Whereas such a message might previously have drawn no response from the United States, Kirkpatrick took action. She sent letters to 66 signers of the communiqué, who represented countries that were moderately friendly to the United States and asked them to explain their support of it. So effective was her letter that a few countries that did not receive her letter protested their exclusion, arguing that they, too, were friendly to the United States and deserved her questioning.

In this bold move, Kirkpatrick signaled, early on in her career as ambassador, that she regarded the UN and the actions of the nonaligned countries with seriousness. Subsequently, U.S. bashing at the UN declined significantly. Later, she reflected on those events. "The Cubans had progressively succeeded in simply enlisting the nonaligned movement in support of Soviet goals," she said. "That communiqué made it sound as though the U.S. was the greatest threat to freedom in the world, and the greatest purveyor of exploitation in the world. There was not a single criticism or negative mention of the Soviet Union, in a year in which the Soviets had invaded Afghanistan.

"I talked to a number of countries in the nonaligned movement," Kirkpatrick said, "who were friends of ours, to see how things worked." Repeatedly, the explanation she heard was that the United States did not care about debate at the UN. To underscore that the United States cared how the nonaligned nations behaved at the UN, Kirkpatrick began sending their voting records to Congress. Her efforts eventually resulted in legislation that linked U.S. foreign aid to recipients' voting patterns at the UN.

But Kirkpatrick's strong stance with the nonaligned nations also drew fire. *Time* magazine published an article entitled "Letter Bomb" on October 26, 1981, stating that "diplomats at the U.N. were atwitter, grumbling that the letter was unmatched in its undiplomatic tone." *Time* also reported that Kirkpatrick's colleagues considered her "schoolmarmish" and "uppity." "Friends and foes alike consider

Alexander Haig resigned as U.S. secretary of state on June 25, 1982. His clashes with Kirkpatrick had made her job particularly difficult. Speaking to the Women's Forum in New York City, she later noted: "I am sure Alexander Haig thought he was going to wipe me out in the first nine months. He didn't."

Kirkpatrick's staff inexperienced and inept." The mistake of her staff, according to *Time*, was that they had not monitored the actions of the non-aligned countries and urged them toward moderation before the communiqué was released.

The same week the *Time* article was published, Kirkpatrick spoke at Arizona State University, where she dismissed the media charges. "Being so categorized in a national magazine is one of the penalties for violating the conventions of the United Nations system," she said.

When Kirkpatrick had completed almost a full year at the UN, she seriously considered resigning. It had been an extremely difficult year. "I was subjected to a lot of harsh criticism in my first year," she said later. In a 1982 interview with the *New York Times*, she said she was "intensely unhappy most of last year." Although she had scored several victories as ambassador, her personal life was suffering. She kept the job, she said, "at almost total cost of my personal life, family, friends, writing, reading, music. The only reason I'm in this job is if I find it do-able, a reasonable chance of being successful." Later she mused, "It's too important a job not to do. My conception of citizenship is to give it the best try you can."

Kirkpatrick later attributed her first-year difficulties to her outsider status at the UN and in the Reagan administration. Not only was she the only woman at the UN who headed a delegation, but she was the only woman who helped forge the country's foreign policy. Additionally, she was not a career diplomat. "The fact that I was from outside the diplomatic world helped to make me particularly unwelcome," she said. "Of course I never could have risen within the diplomatic world, to that level. Any woman who became ambassador would have had to come from the outside."

Kirkpatrick discussed the possibility of resigning with her husband, her three sons, and her brother. They all urged her to stay. In a later interview with *Working Woman*, Kirkpatrick said she learned, after her first year, to delegate more responsibility. "My first approach," she said, "was to try to learn everything about a subject and do everything. Read everything, write everything, decide everything. And that was an important phase of learning the job for me. Now, though, I've developed habits and patterns of delegation and a

A stark photograph reveals Kirkpatrick looking out over Masada, Israel, on her first official trip as ambassador. Her steadfast support of Israel led to a difficult situation at the beginning of her term at the UN, during the vote of condemnation for Israel's bombing of an Iraqi nuclear facility. Never afraid to take an unpopular position, she ended her tenure supporting the Reagan administration's controversial policy on the contras and Sandinistas in Nicaragua.

A photograph of a briefing of the National Security Council reveals Kirkpatrick, seated on the right side, third from the rear—the only woman there. She once commented, "I was a very big shock to the foreign policy community."

team in which I have a high degree of confidence. I do a great deal of delegating." One person she now relied on was Susan Johnson, a career diplomat, whom Kirkpatrick appointed to keep track of the activities of the nonaligned nations.

An event in the summer of 1982 also helped her do her job more effectively. On June 25, Alexander Haig resigned as secretary of state after another skir- mish with Kirkpatrick. In April, when Argentina invaded the Falkland Islands, Haig had first directed Kirkpatrick to veto a resolution about the crisis; then he told her to abstain. The UN does not allow such switches, but Kirkpatrick issued a statement saying that the United States would change its vote, if that were possible. The whole incident made Kirkpatrick appear incompetent, and she was embarrassed by it. President Reagan, too, was reportedly bothered by Haig's signal switching. Soon after, Reagan accepted Haig's resignation.

With the new secretary of state, George P. Shultz, Kirkpatrick's work proceeded more smoothly. One area where she continued to have a strong impact was in U.S. relations with Latin America, especially Nicaragua. Here, Reagan adopted the so-called Kirkpatrick Doctrine, which called for U.S. support of the anti-Sandinista fighters, known as the contras, who were trying to destabilize the Communist government of the Sandinistas. As a member of the National Security Planning Group—which includes several members of the National Security Council but is smaller—Kirkpatrick supported the decision to supply the contras with covert, or secret, aid. She was convinced that the contras could not win without U.S. aid and that if they did not win, other countries in Latin America would also become Communist.

On March 1, 1982, Kirkpatrick testified before a Senate subcommittee on human rights in Nicaragua. She said that under the Sandinistas, Nicaragua had no free press—other than one newspaper—and that it was a crime there to criticize the government without permission. The Sandinistas, she said, had postponed elections and had "moved against labor as well as business, fiercely attacking Nicaragua's independent trade union movement."

Later in the month, Kirkpatrick answered charges made by Daniel Ortega, the leader of the Sandinistas, to the UN. Ortega had told the UN that the United States was about to launch an invasion into Nicaragua. Kirkpatrick responded, "But, of course, that is ridiculous. The U.S. government is not about to invade anyone. And we have so stated on many occasions." The United States sought peace in Nicaragua, Kirkpatrick said. The Sandinistas, she said, not the United States, were the ones guilty of aggression. She outlined evidence that the Sandinistas were supplying military aid to revolutionary guerrilla fighters in El Salvador and that the Cubans were supplying more and more military advisers to Nicaragua.

At Reagan's request, Kirkpatrick traveled to Latin America in 1983, returning with recommendations that he adopted. She advocated considerably more aid to the contras and American support for peace talks. Reagan could not convince Congress, however, to grant more aid to the contras. In 1984—after learning that the harbors of Nicaragua had been mined with explosives by presidential order—Congress cut off all aid to the contras. Kirkpatrick later said she would have opposed the mining of Nicaraguan ports but that it was never discussed in meetings of the National Security Planning Group.

For the next several years, long after she left the UN, Kirkpatrick would continue commenting on the Sandinista government and the progress of peace talks. When the Iran-contra scandal broke in late 1986—revealing that officials in the National Security Council had secretly sold arms to Iranian terrorists and used the proceeds to support the contras—Kirkpatrick would describe what she thought had gone wrong. She believed that Congress had overstepped its bounds by cutting off aid to the contras and thus trying to take charge of foreign policy. The president, she argued, was the principal agent of foreign policy, not the Congress. By prohibiting aid to the contras, the Congress had laid the groundwork for the National Security Council's secret mission, she claimed.

At the same time Kirkpatrick was helping to shape U.S. foreign policy, the AEI was publishing two new books she had written. In 1982, a collection of her essays appeared, including, and carrying the title of, her famous article "Dictatorships and Double Standards." The book was reviewed, somewhat unfavorably, on the front page of the *New York Times*. A year later, a collection of her speeches on foreign policy was published, entitled *The Reagan Phenomenon*. In it Kirkpatrick outlined what she meant by "the Reagan Phenomenon": "The restoration of the conviction that American power is necessary for the survival of liberal democracy in the modern world."

She returned to this theme in August 1984, when she traveled to Dallas to address the Republican National Convention on Reagan's behalf: "Today, foreign policy is central to the security, to the freedom, to the prosperity, even to the survival of the United States. And *our* strength, for which we make many sacrifices, is essential to the independence and freedom of our allies and of our friends."

By late 1984, Kirkpatrick was ready to resign from the UN. She had accomplished her goal of improving U.S. influence, and there were fewer attacks on the United States by the small, nonaligned nations. In her interview with Fasulo, Kirkpatrick noted that when the General Assembly voted negatively on the issue of the colonial status of Puerto Rico, "it was our first clear voting victory, the first vote that the United States has won in the General Assembly for more than a decade." The world knew that the United States was serious about diplomacy at the UN. Kirkpatrick also felt she had served long enough. She explained in a later interview; "In a democracy, I think if a president asks you to serve, unless there's some really overwhelming counter-duty, then I think one has an obligation to serve and give it one's best effort. I had given the U.N. my very best effort. I took my turn."

She had served more than four years, longer than any UN ambassador since Adlai Stevenson. The rapid turnover that preceded her had contributed, she believed, to the decline in U.S. influence. "The job is terribly difficult and frustrating," she wrote. "Nonetheless, in principle, we ought to have representatives who stay there long enough to know the scene." She had learned the scene and, she believed, improved U.S. standing within it. She wanted to go home, to her husband and Georgetown University.

Kirkpatrick's husband was ill, and she was finding it intolerable to be away from him. She also wanted to return to Georgetown, where she held an endowed chair—a professorship named after a benefactor of the college that carries extra privileges and salary. Georgetown had granted her an indefinite leave, but she felt it unfair to the university to stay on at the UN.

Kirkpatrick now wanted to return to private life. She told an interviewer from *Newsweek*, "A scholar and writer is what I have wanted to be all my life. I think it's the most interesting, even exciting, thing to be."

Assessments of her achievements were mainly laudatory. A columnist for *Time* magazine wrote: "Jeane Kirkpatrick left her mark on foreign policy.

Sir Anthony Parsons, British ambassador to the UN, and Kirkpatrick share a rare moment of levity during an emergency session of the UN Security Council, which was concerned with the 1982 Falkland Islands crisis.

On January 30, 1985, Kirkpatrick announced her resignation after serving as ambassador to the UN for four years. She looked forward to her return to private life but noted in an interview with Newsweek, "I believe that if one is called upon to spend a reasonable period of one's life in public service in a democracy, that one has a kind of obligation to do so."

Something more. She served with the political enemy—the Republicans. She flourished as a remnant of a tradition that has seen this nation through hard times before." Another writer, in *Business Week*, said, "A sea change has taken place in the way the U.S. treats the U.N. From the outset, Kirkpatrick determined to 'let everybody else understand that the U.S. believes that what happens [at the UN] matters, that we notice, and we care.' "

Shortly before she left the UN, she asserted her belief that the United States should maintain its economic and military strength. However, "force must only be used in extreme cases. If you happen to be the mother of three 'war age' sons, then you think a lot about it. I do believe that having sons affects the way one thinks about war, or concretizes it." Kirkpatrick continued to use all her experiences—personal, political, and intellectual—in arriving at her views and analyses. Although she had left high office, she was about to find a wider audience for her thoughts.

On March 26, 1985, Kirkpatrick gave her final press conference as ambassador at the U.S. mission to the UN. Despite widespread speculation that she would run for office, she steadfastly declined to do so, although she later admitted, "I find it very hard to disengage [from politics]. It's more difficult than I expected it to be. So I haven't."

EIGHT

Commentator on International Events

A few days after she left the UN, Kirkpatrick officially changed her voting registration to Republican and was warmly welcomed to the party. Almost immediately, she was mentioned as a possible candidate for president in 1988. Having served two terms, Reagan could not run for reelection, and as one writer put it in *Newsweek*, "A significant sect within the Republican church wants her to run for president, straight away." Not only Republicans found her an attractive candidate; feminist leaders, regardless of their party affiliation, admired her as well.

Judy Goldsmith, then president of the National Organization for Women (NOW), told a reporter from *Time*: "Whether she is a Democrat or a Republican is not relevant to NOW. She is an ERA [Equal Rights Amendment] supporter and an asset wherever she goes and under whatever cloak she wears." Donna E. Shalala, a liberal Democrat and former president of Hunter College in New York City (she later became president of the University of Wisconsin–Madison), told the *New York Times*, "Jeane is extraordinarily complex. She has a strong commitment to women's issues, a real sensitivity, and I like her. It would be very tough for me to vote for her, because of her international views. But I'd think about it—I wouldn't just knee-jerk, 'No.' "

Despite the widespread interest, Kirkpatrick declined to run. She had meant it when she said she wanted to return to private life. However, many politicians and party officials began to mention the possibility of her becoming secretary of state in a new administration.

Kirkpatrick was relieved to be back in Washington with her family and longtime friends. In 1981, her husband had retired from the American Political Science Association, where he had served for 25 years, but kept his position as president of the Helen Dwight Reid Educational Foundation, where he had served in various capacities since 1960, and his position as chairman of trustees at the Institute of American Universities in France. Kirkpatrick rejoined him, relaxing in the house they had lived in for 30 years, away from the noise of international conflicts. That summer, she and her husband traveled again to France, where they now had a house near the small town of Saint-Rémy-de-Provence, a town known for its flowers, sun, and sparkling fountain. The small-town girl from the American Midwest had found another small town as her second home.

When she returned from France, Kirkpatrick came back to a very public private life. She returned to Georgetown and the AEI and also began writing a weekly column on international affairs for the Los Angeles Times syndicate, a column published in more than 100 U.S. newspapers and 30 foreign papers. Before she left the UN, the State Department had made an unsuccessful attempt to censor her writing, but Kirkpatrick would have none of that.

She had willingly signed releases stating that she would not reveal any classified, or secret, information after she left her government job. But when another release appeared on her desk—one that would allow the State Department to approve or reject anything she

wrote pertaining to foreign policy—she said no. "You can't write a column and put it through a State Department clearance process," she said later. Fortunately, her refusal to sign the document did not cause problems. Somehow, though, news of the incident reached the media. Although her stand earned her widespread praise, even among her critics, she firmly stated, "I certainly didn't make it public. I never would have made it public."

She did, of course, continue to make public her views on foreign events. Along with her books, articles, and speeches, her column became the platform from which she spoke, commenting on a variety of topics——from new developments in the Soviet Union and Eastern Europe to U.S. presidential elections.

At about the time Kirkpatrick left the UN, a new Soviet leader came to power. In March 1985, Mikhail S. Gorbachev was chosen general secretary of the Soviet Communist party, ending an era of stagnation in Soviet politics and ushering in a wave of reforms, including *perestroika* (restructuring) and *glasnost* (openness). With Gorbachev's ascension, U.S.-Soviet relations improved; in 1987, the two countries signed an arms control treaty. Gorbachev began allowing the Soviet people more freedom, and the Soviet Union relaxed its grip on Eastern European countries such as Poland and Hungary, allowing them to establish new governments elected by their people.

In February 1987, Kirkpatrick met with Gorbachev at the Kremlin, the

An Afghan man presents a departing Soviet soldier with flowers in May 1988. Kirkpatrick had condemned the Soviet Union's 1981 invasion of Afghanistan; she greeted the massive withdrawal of Soviet troops with approval.

headquarters of Soviet government, in Moscow. As part of a small group from the Council on Foreign Relations, a U.S. organization that tries to improve understanding of American foreign policy and international affairs, Kirkpatrick traveled to Moscow with other former government officials, including Henry Kissinger, who served as secretary of state under President Nixon. The group talked with Gorbachev for three hours. "He was a very impressive man," she said later, "with great political skills and authentic charisma, which you don't see too often." In her column, published in the *Washington Post*, she speculated on why Gorbachev was permitting the Soviet people more religious freedom and allowing previously banned books to be published. "The most likely reason, I believe, is that Gorbachev has decided that totalitarian control is not compatible with modernization," she wrote, "and is not necessary to continued political control by the Communist Party."

When the Soviet Union held elections in 1989—for the first time in 70 years—Communist party chiefs in 6 major cities were unseated. Although most candidates in the election were Communist, which made the voting only partly free, the very existence of elections was a move toward democracy. In a 1989 interview, Kirkpatrick reflected on whether multiparty elections might eventually occur in the Soviet Union. "In a way, they already have," she said. "What has happened in places like Latvia, Lithuania, and Esto-

After a day of shopping in West Berlin, East Berlin youths return home with a new radio–cassette player—nearly impossible to buy in their own part of the city. As the physical and political division between East and West Germany was dismantled, East Germans welcomed the opportunity to purchase goods unavailable in their country, but more important, they welcomed free elections and a free press.

nia is that opposition groups based on nationalist ethnic groups are functioning as parties." (The Baltic states of Latvia, Lithuania, and Estonia were annexed by the Soviet Union during World II; in the 1989 elections, voters in those states supported their ethnic representatives.)

Outside of its borders, the Soviet Union was also ending its aggressive policies. It once claimed the right to invade another country if the stability of a Communist government was threatened. In 1981, for example, it had invaded Afghanistan to bolster the Communist regime there. In 1988, though, Gorbachev began withdrawing Soviet troops from Afghanistan. In her column, Kirkpatrick gave her views on the withdrawal, saying Gorbachev was trying to "improve his overall strategic position." He did not want the Soviet Union perceived as aggressive against other countries.

In Eastern Europe, as well, the new Soviet policy was to let Communist states choose their own future. When the people of Hungary rose against their Communist government in 1956, the Soviets invaded and violently repressed the uprising. In the late 1980s, however, the Hungarian government promoted democratic reforms, and the Soviet Union did not object.

One of the most dramatic changes in Eastern Europe occurred in East Germany, when the Communist party there announced sweeping changes in the government, including free elections, separation of the party and state, and new freedom-of-assembly laws. On November 9, 1989, the Berlin Wall was opened, and hundreds of thousands of East Berliners streamed into West Berlin. By September 1990, the Berlin Wall had been demolished, and on October 3, the East German parliament voted to dissolve itself and its nation and join West Germany to become one nation— the Federal Republic of Germany. Two months later, on December 2, in the first elections held throughout all of Germany since World War II, Germans chose a government to run their reunified nation. The face of Europe changed profoundly.

The government of Poland, too, which had been Communist since the end of World War II, moved toward democracy. The Polish trade union Solidarity, which mobilized sentiment against communism, was outlawed in 1981. By 1989, though, Solidarity had gained control of the government after Poland's most open elections in 40 years. Again, the Soviet Union did not interfere. Kirkpatrick reflected on these events in her column, writing in the *Washington Post*, "In fact, no one knows how much freedom or independence Soviet leaders will tolerate. But in Hungary, Poland and Lithuania, governments and dissidents are testing the limits."

Closer to home, the Sandinista government in Nicaragua, which was backed by the Soviets and Cubans, was also undergoing change. In the summer of 1987, Sandinista leader Daniel Ortega signed a peace plan that provided for free elections and a free press. The country had been racked by civil war

99

for years, as the contras fought government forces. Popular sentiment against the Sandinista government grew. The anti-Sandinistas chose Violeta Chamorro as their candidate in the presidential elections scheduled for 1990. In a 1989 interview, Kirkpatrick gave her assessment of Chamorro: "She's a wonderful, dynamic, exciting person, with a great deal of courage." Did Kirkpatrick think Chamorro had a chance at the presidency? "I don't know. I hope so," she said. "That depends on the restraint of the Sandinista government in the use of force. I am very skeptical about the Ortega brothers' [Daniel Ortega's brother was also a member of the Sandinista government] restraint in the use of force. But I have almost total confidence that given a free choice the people of Nicaragua would overwhelmingly defeat the Sandinista government."

In December 1989, a team of UN observers in Nicaragua to monitor the electoral process reported that violence and inflammatory news coverage—by both the Sandinista government and the opposition—could threaten the prospects of a free, fair election. Nevertheless, the election proceeded in early 1990, and Chamorro won by a narrow margin. On April 25, 1990, she was inaugurated president, and shortly thereafter, President George Bush signed a declaration that Nicaragua was no longer a Communist country, which allowed the war-ravaged nation to receive U.S. aid.

Asked whether her ideas about totalitarianism had changed since she wrote her famous *Commentary* article, Kirkpatrick said, "Yes, they are updated. I said we had no example in history of a totalitarian regime being transformed from within. But the transformation in the Soviet Union has already gone further than any totalitarian regime ever has." Hungary and Poland were different, she said, because in those countries totalitarian regimes had not arisen within the country but were imposed from outside.

One totalitarian government that was not moving toward democracy in the late 1980s was China. In the summer of 1989, Chinese students holding prodemocracy demonstrations were crushed in a military massacre. Kirkpatrick said of this event: "It was sheer tragedy. That was an example of a government using the force available to it. All governments have an overwhelming advantage in instrumentalities of force. Democracy exists where governments are restrained in the use of force."

Back in the United States, when the Republicans chose Vice-president George Bush as their presidential candidate in 1988, Kirkpatrick traveled to the national convention in New Orleans and again brought Republicans to their feet with her speech. She criticized the Democrats, saying their "basic approach hasn't changed since George McGovern was nominated in 1972 and since Jimmy Carter was elected in 1976." After eight years of Reagan, she said, "American relations with the Soviet Union have never been better. . . . Some of this improvement

Violeta Chamorro (first row, second from left) raises her arms in victory after winning Nicaragua's presidential election on February 28, 1990. Kirkpatrick doubted the Sandinistas would allow themselves to be defeated in free elections but was pleasantly surprised by the outcome.

reflects the results of a new Soviet leader with some different ideas. But much of it is due to the restored strength and purpose and confidence and skill and persistence of the United States."

Criticizing the Democratic candidate, Michael Dukakis, for being weak on military defense, she said his "ideas about defense differ sharply from past Republican and Democratic administrations since World War II. Unlike any of them, he believes that conventional forces can be a substitute for nuclear deterrents. . . . Michael Dukakis simply doesn't take the need for defense seriously."

Later, in her weekly column Kirkpatrick explained why she thought Bush was leading in the polls against Michael Dukakis. "In cultural politics Michael Dukakis has become a metaphor for the attitudes Americans reject every time they get the chance." Americans did not want—had not wanted since George McGovern, she believed —a president who was a "cultural liberal." In her view, Americans wanted a president who represented traditional values—in this case, George Bush.

Bush won the 1988 election easily, carrying all but 10 states and the District of Columbia. Kirkpatrick offered him some advice in an article she wrote

Republicans cheer for George Bush at the 1988 Republican National Convention. Kirkpatrick's speech there elicited a standing ovation from the crowd.

for *National Review* magazine. Here, voicing her concerns with domestic issues, she sounded almost like a liberal Democrat, urging Bush to "provide more and better child care and early-childhood education, to raise educational standards and the quality of public education, to protect young Americans against drugs and the drug culture. Other industrial nations have found ways to accomplish these tasks and also to ensure that health care and shelter are provided for all citizens. Surely we can too." But her advice on

foreign policy remained in line with conservatives of both parties, concerned with what she said was the growing military vulnerability of the United States.

By 1990, Kirkpatrick thoroughly enjoyed having more control over her time than she had at the UN. On a typical weekday, she reluctantly gets up at 6:30 A.M., showers, and shampoos. While drinking a pot of tea, she reads the Washington and national newspapers. Then she leaves the house for her offices at Georgetown or the AEI; normally, she spends two days a week at Georgetown, where one of the courses she teaches is concerned with "political personality"—the importance of the personal qualities and character of politicians. Or she might have a meeting at the White House of the president's Foreign Intelligence Advisory Board, on which she has served since she left the UN. This group, which includes Henry Kissinger and Zbigniew Brzezinski, a former U.S. national security adviser, meets for a couple of days every two months to examine the adequacy of U.S. foreign intelligence—the information available to U.S. diplomats and policymakers about events in the rest of the world.

Another government board on which Kirkpatrick serves is the Defense Policy Review Board. This group, composed of "defense intellectuals," looks at how the Department of Defense is doing in its assessments of strategy and preparation. Kirkpatrick's service on both of these boards is strictly as a volunteer. "You not only don't get any compensation," she said, "you buy your own lunch."

If she does not have a meeting of one of these government boards, Kirkpatrick might be attending a board meeting of the Council on Foreign Relations. She is a director of the council and serves on its executive committee, a post she has held since 1985. The council takes no political position on foreign-policy issues but promotes the exchange of ideas, often hosting conferences that feature speakers from foreign countries.

At the AEI, Kirkpatrick meets with students, research assistants, and foreign visitors; one 1990 visitor was a former head of the Soviet foreign ministry. At lunchtime, she might have a meeting to attend where she may or may not be giving a speech. One luncheon was a gathering of "Washington's 100 most powerful women." "I enjoyed that," Kirkpatrick said later. "I think it's important for women who are influential to know each other."

After lunch, Kirkpatrick is back at the office, where she works until seven or seven-thirty in the evening, unless she leaves early for a speaking engagement. Usually she speaks to academic or political groups—such as a conference on the Israeli constitution or a meeting of donors to the Republican party—for which she refuses to accept fees. However, she has an agent who arranges for her less-frequent corporate appearances, and Kirkpatrick receives substantial fees for those occasions, which have included several speeches to IBM executives.

When she is at home in the evening, Kirkpatrick has dinner with her husband. Their live-in housekeeper usually prepares the meal, although Kirkpatrick loves to cook. Sometimes friends join the Kirkpatricks for dinner, or their sons drop in for a visit.

Kirkpatrick's eldest and middle sons are attorneys—Douglas, the oldest, works in publishing; John, the middle son, is in a law firm. Her youngest son, Stuart, is in graduate school pursuing east Asian studies. Her first grandchild, Laura, was born in 1986 to her son John and his wife. "We finally got a girl in our family," Kirkpatrick said of her granddaughter, "and she's beautiful." Her sons and their families visit often, both in Washington and in France.

During her summers in the south of France, Kirkpatrick spends her time reading, writing, and cooking. She particularly enjoys food shopping in the daily markets. "Living here is an aesthetic experience," she told a reporter from *W* magazine. "You can't find these colors, tastes, smells and light anywhere else in the world." The outdoor markets at St. Rémy-de-Provence, Arles, and Maussane are her favorites, and she told *W* how much she likes to mingle with the French shoppers, carefully choosing ripe melons by their aroma. "It's inspiring, even if you're not a painter, to see the different fruits come and go. In France one cooks by the season, and that's the greatest luxury for anyone who loves food."

Although her cooking skills declined during her years at the UN, they had fully returned by the summer of 1989.

At the age of 65 in 1991, Kirkpatrick had no plans to retire and remained very much in the public eye. As an esteemed Georgetown professor, a member of several governmental advisory boards, the author of a syndicated newspaper column, and an international affairs analyst on television discussion programs, she can speak from a unique perspective, for she was the only woman to have attained a position of power in U.S. foreign policy in the 1980s.

"My cooking got back up to par for the first time since I went to the U.N.," Kirkpatrick said. "You have to do it to get it right, and I did a lot of it this summer. But I don't have the time for it in a normal day."

A normal day for Kirkpatrick might seem exhausting to others. In addition to her academic, consulting, and governmental responsibilities, she is much sought after as a guest on talk shows about foreign affairs. When Iraq invaded and overran Kuwait in August 1990, Kirkpatrick was on vacation. Upon her return to the United States, she appeared on the Cable News Network (CNN), was interviewed on the public-television program "American Interests," and as a guest on a number of other news and discussion shows offered her analysis of the Iraqi situation and her thoughts about the proper U.S. response. Her opinions remain widely respected, not only regarding foreign policy. On September 10, 1990, on the television program "Firing Line," she debated the question, "Resolved: Government is not the solution to the problem; it is the problem." She argued for the Republican side with William F. Buckley, Jr., and Charlton Heston against the Democratic team of Gary Hart, Pat Schroeder, Dennis Weaver, and George McGovern.

Since she left the UN, she has also been working on two books: one on how the UN operates and another on the changes in the Soviet Union and Eastern Europe. When she has a chance, she reads fiction—Saul Bellow's novel *A Theft*, for example. At age 65, Kirkpatrick is relaxed but productive and still going strong. When an interviewer asked whether she had any plans to retire, she said firmly, "Of course not."

Whatever Kirkpatrick chooses to do in the coming years, she will undoubtedly bring all her varied experience to bear on the task at hand. One of her favorite stories comes from her days as a member of the National Security Planning Group. She told a *New York Times* reporter that the group assembled in the Situation Room was startled by the appearance of a mouse heading toward the table they were gathered around. "A mouse? A mouse in the Situation Room?" was their incredulous response. Kirkpatrick recalls musing, "That mouse is no more surprising a creature to see in the Situation Room than I am—no stranger a presence here, really, than I am." Kirkpatrick's presence has been surprising in many areas: as a woman in the male world of foreign policy, as a former staunch Democrat among Republicans, as a professor in the UN, and as a former small-town resident consulted about world politics. At the end of her entry in *Who's Who in America*, Kirkpatrick concludes with the following note: "My experience demonstrates to my satisfaction that it is both possible and feasible for women in our times to successfully combine traditional and professional roles, that it is not necessary to ape men's career patterns . . . instead, one can do quite different things at different stages of one's life. All that is required is a little luck and a lot of work."

FURTHER READING

Kaiser, Charles. *1968 in America: Music, Politics, Chaos, Counterculture and the Shaping of a Generation.* New York: Weidenfeld & Nicolson, 1988.

Kirkpatrick, Jeane J. *Dictatorships and Double Standards: Rationalism and Reason in Politics.* New York: Simon & Schuster and the American Enterprise Institute for Public Policy Research, 1982.

———. *Leader and Vanguard in Mass Society: A Study of Peronist Argentina.* Cambridge: The MIT Press, 1971.

———. *The New Presidential Elite: Men and Women in National Politics.* New York: Russell Sage Foundation and the Twentieth-century Fund, 1976.

———. *Political Woman.* New York: Basic Books, 1974.

———. *The Reagan Doctrine and U.S. Foreign Policy.* Washington, DC: The Heritage Foundation, 1985.

———. *The Reagan Phenomenon: And Other Speeches on Foreign Policy.* Washington and London: American Enterprise Institute for Public Policy Research, 1983.

———, ed. *The Strategy of Deception: A Study in World-wide Communist Tactics.* New York: Farrar, Straus & Giroux, 1963.

Neumann, Franz. *Behemoth: The Structure and Practice of National Socialism 1933–1944.* New York: Oxford University Press, 1942.

CHRONOLOGY

Nov. 19, 1926	Jeane Duane Jordan born in Duncan, Oklahoma
1938	Jordan family moves to Vandalia, Illinois
1940	Jordan family moves to Mount Vernon, Illinois
1944	Jordan enrolls at Stephens College in Columbia, Missouri
1946	Earns Associate of Arts degree from Stephens; enrolls at Barnard College in New York
1948	Earns B.A. in political science from Barnard; enrolls at Columbia University
1950	Earns M.A. in political science from Columbia
1951	Works as research analyst at the Department of State in Washington, D.C.
1952–53	Does postgraduate work at the Institute de Science Politique of the University of Paris under a fellowship from the French government
1953–54	Works as assistant to the director of the Economic Cooperation Administration in Washington, D.C.
1954–56	Works as research associate with the Human Resources Research Office of George Washington University
1955	Marries Dr. Evron M. Kirkpatrick
1956	First son, Douglas Jordan, born on July 17
1956–58	Kirkpatrick works part-time as research associate for the "Communism in Government" project of the Fund for the Republic
1958	Second son, John Evron, born on March 13
1959	Third son, Stuart Alan, born on September 19
1962	Kirkpatrick appointed assistant professor of political science at Trinity College in Washington, D.C.
1967	Appointed associate professor of political science at Georgetown University
1968	Earns Ph.D. in political science from Columbia University
1971	*Leader and Vanguard in Mass Society* is published
1972	Kirkpatrick helps form the Coalition for a Democratic Majority, a group of Democrats dubbed neoconservatives
1974	*Political Woman* is published
1976	*The New Presidential Elite* is published
1977	Kirkpatrick appointed senior fellow at the American Enterprise Institute
1979	"Dictatorships and Double Standards" is published in *Commentary* magazine
1980	Kirkpatrick appointed permanent ambassador to the United Nations
1982	*Dictatorships and Double Standards* is published
1983	*The Reagan Phenomenon* is published
1985	Kirkpatrick resigns post at the UN and changes party affiliation to Republican; begins writing a syndicated column on international affairs for the Los Angeles Times Syndicate

INDEX

Pat Harrison, a native of Oklahoma, received her B.A. in English from the University of Oklahoma in 1971 and her M.F.A. in fiction from Sarah Lawrence College. She is a senior fund-raising writer at Brigham and Women's Hospital in Boston.

❖   ❖   ❖

Matina S. Horner is president emerita of Radcliffe College and associate professor of psychology and social relations at Harvard University. She is best known for her studies of women's motivation, achievement, and personality development. Dr. Horner serves on several national boards and advisory councils, including those of the National Science Foundation, Time Inc., and the Women's Research and Education Institute. She earned her B.A. from Bryn Mawr College and Ph.D. from the University of Michigan, and holds honorary degrees from many colleges and universities, including Mount Holyoke, Smith, Tufts, and the University of Pennsylvania.